The House of Windsor
Denis Judd

The House of Windsor

Denis Judd

Macdonald · London

© This arrangement of photographs:
Conway Picture Library 1973

© Text: Denis Judd 1973

Picture research by Alan Smith

First published in Great Britain in 1973 by
Macdonald & Jane's
St Giles House
49 Poland Street
London W1

ISBN (cloth) 0 356 04571 4
ISBN (paper) 0 356 04735 0

Made and printed in Great Britain by
Morrison & Gibb Ltd
London and Edinburgh

FRONTISPIECE: Windsor Castle in Berkshire – apt symbol of English history and the newly named royal house

Contents

The Royal Circle

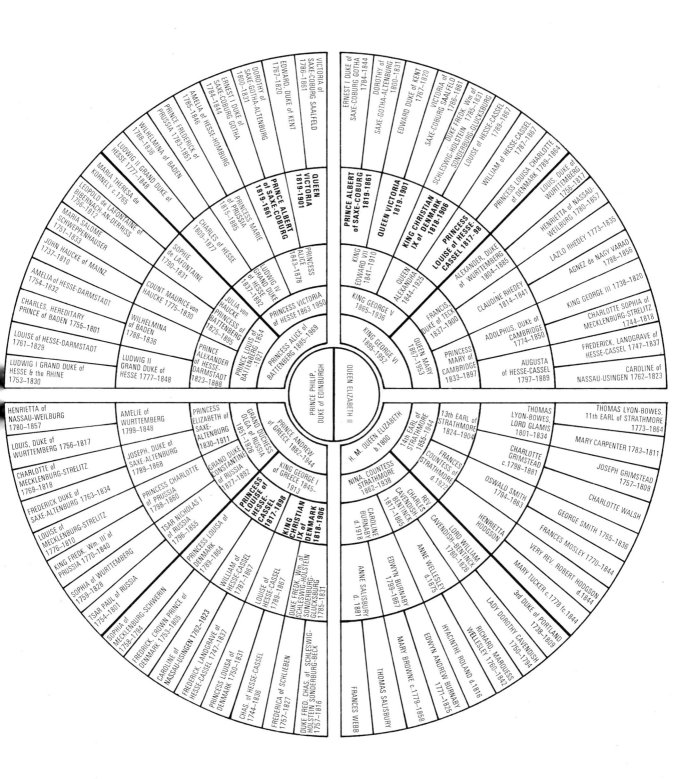

The House of Windsor

GEORGE V
1910–1936
(became first sovereign of the House of Windsor 1917)
= PRINCESS MARY of Teck (d. 1953) (H.M. Queen Mary)

EDWARD VIII
1936
(became Duke of Windsor) (d. 1972)
= Mrs WALLIS WARFIELD (Mrs Simpson) (m. 1937)

GEORGE VI
1936–1952
= Lady ELIZABETH BOWES-LYON (H.M. Queen Elizabeth, the Queen Mother) (m. 1923)

H.R.H. Prince HENRY Duke of Gloucester, K.G. (b. 1900)
= Lady ALICE MONTAGU-DOUGLAS-SCOTT, (m. 1935)

H.R.H. Prince WILLIAM of Gloucester (1941-72)

H.R.H. Prince RICHARD of Gloucester (b. 1944)

H.M. Queen ELIZABETH II
(b. April 21, 1926,
m. Nov. 20, 1947)
Ascended the Throne, Feb. 6, 1952
= H.R.H. The Prince PHILIP Duke of Edinburgh, K.G. (b. 1921)

H.R.H. The Prince CHARLES Prince of Wales, K.G. (Heir Apparent to the Throne) (b. Nov. 14, 1948)

H.R.H. The Prince ANDREW (b. 1960)

H.R.H. The Prince EDWARD (b. 1964)

H.R.H. The Princess ANNE (b. 1950)
= Capt. MARK PHILLIPS (m. Nov. 1973)

H.R.H. The Princess MARGARET (b. 1930, m. 1960)
= ANTONY ARMSTRONG-JONES 1st Earl of Snowdon

DAVID Viscount Linley (b. 1961)

Lady SARAH (b. 1964)

H.R.H. Prince GEORGE Duke of Kent, K.G. (1902-42)
= H.R.H. Princess MARINA of Greece (m. 1934, d. 1968)

H.R.H. Prince JOHN (1905-19)

H.R.H. Princess MARY (Princess Royal) (b. 1897, m. 1922, d. 1965)
= HENRY LASCELLES 6th Earl of Harewood, K.G. (d. 1947)

KATHARINE WORSLEY (m. 1961)
= H.R.H. Prince EDWARD Duke of Kent (b. 1935)

H.R.H. Prince MICHAEL of Kent (b. 1942)

H.R.H. Princess ALEXANDRA of Kent (b. 1936)
= Hon. ANGUS OGILVY (m. 1963)

JAMES (b. 1964)

MARINA (b. 1966)

GEORGE Earl of St. Andrews (b. 1962)

Lord NICHOLAS WINDSOR (b. 1970)

Lady HELEN WINDSOR (b. 1964)

GEORGE LASCELLES 7th Earl of Harewood (b. 1923)
= MARIA DONATA (MARION) STEIN (m. 1949, div. 1967) = 2ndly Patricia Tuckwell (m. 1967)

Hon. GERALD LASCELLES (b. 1924)
= ANGELA DOWDING (m. 1952)

Henry (b. 1953)

DAVID Viscount Lascelles (b. 1950)

Hon. JAMES (b. 1953)

Hon. JEREMY (b. 1955)

Hon. MARK (b. 1964)

Preface

It is exactly a thousand years since the Anglo-Saxon ruler Edgar was crowned King of all England. Between 973 and 1973 fifty-one monarchs have occupied the throne and have included saints, lechers, madmen, tyrants, reformers, soldiers of genius, consummate diplomats, homosexuals, debauchees, staid family men and women, bunglers, fools, philosophers and theologians. Royal house has succeeded royal house, from Anglo-Saxon and Dane to Norman, Plantagenet, Lancaster, York, Tudor, Stuart, Hanover, Saxe-Coburg-Gotha and, finally, Windsor.

The House of Windsor has been established for more than half a century. During those years, two World Wars and innumerable smaller conflicts have taken place; there have been throughout the world revolutions and counter-revolutions, race-riots and class warfare; societies in every quarter of the globe have experienced startling changes and sometimes uncomfortable convulsions; the visual arts, literature, public entertainments, fashions, social habits, methods of communication and national mores have been transformed; old empires have been lost and new ideals of international cooperation found.

Yet while republics multiply and Scandinavian monarchies democratize in earnest, the House of Windsor retains both its mystique and its rapport with its subjects. Its durability owes something to the conservatism of the British people and something to the integrity of the three monarchs who have dominated its history: George V, George VI and Elizabeth II. Even the brief, awkward and divisive reign of Edward VIII was preceded by the distinguished if controversial service of that monarch, as Prince of Wales, to his people and his times.

During the decade of the 1970s there have been, and will be, opportunities to reflect upon the special relationship that exists between the British royal house and the public: in November 1972 the Queen and Prince Philip celebrated their Silver Wedding; in February 1973 the Queen had reigned for twenty-one years, and in November 1973 Princess Anne marries Captain Mark Phillips; in June 1974 twenty-one years will have passed since Queen Elizabeth's coronation; and she will also be able to celebrate her Silver Jubilee in February 1977, twenty-five years after her accession to the throne. It is a safe prediction that though some critics will complain of a 'royal soap opera', the House of Windsor will acquit itself with its customary dignity and decorum during these commemorations.

Why Windsor?
In August 1914 the British Empire went to war with Imperial Germany and Austria–Hungary, and earlier, somewhat romantic, hopes that Anglo-Saxon and Teuton could cooperate in an orderly global supervision of lesser breeds lay in ruins. Instead of the *Pax*

1 The old order was about to change. George V, wearing the uniform of a German general, visits Berlin in May 1913 and rides with his cousin, the Kaiser, whom he was shortly to strip of all English military honours

Teutonica the world witnessed four years of horrendous slaughter culminating in Bolshevik revolution and the redrawing of the map of Europe, as well as of the Middle East.

In Britain official phlegm contrasted bizarrely with hysterical public outbursts of anti-German feeling. East End shops bearing German-sounding names were ransacked, and, at a more exalted level, King George V was pressed by over-zealous patriots to expunge the names of the Kaiser and his heir the Crown Prince, who both held the honorary command of British regiments, from the Army List; other equally trivial and irrational demands followed.

Amid this atmosphere of petty suspicions and vituperative innuendoes the title of the British royal house, Saxe-Coburg-Gotha, stood out like a sore thumb. In 1917 H. G. Wells, novelist, socialist, and scientific seer, referred disparagingly to an 'alien and uninspiring court'. George V, who could quite happily have spent his whole life as a Norfolk squire or a naval officer, replied robustly: 'I may be uninspiring, but I'll be damned if I'm an alien.' Still, there was a distinctly Germanic whiff about the royal house: the King's German grand-father, Prince Albert, had brought the ponderous 'Saxe-Coburg-Gotha' in his wake when he married Queen Victoria in 1840; King Edward VII, King George V's father, had a guttural pronunciation and had rolled his r's with rrrelish; the family was connected by close blood links not only to the German royal house of Hohenzollern-Sigmaringen, but also to a number of lesser German princes.

It therefore seemed expedient in 1917 to seek a new name for the British royal family. But what name? The Royal College of Heralds toyed with 'Guelph', then suggested that either 'Wipper' or 'Wettin' could properly be adopted; happily, the King rejected these proposals. Neither 'Tudor' nor 'Stuart' had unblemished associations; 'Plantaganet', 'York', 'Lancaster', 'England', and 'Fitzroy' were finally considered unacceptable.

Lord Stamfordham, King George's Private Secretary, then dug up 'Windsor'. Edward III had apparently been called 'Edward of Windsor' at one time; Rudyard Kipling had hailed Queen Victoria as the 'Widow at Windsor' in his verse; above all, 'Windsor' was so English, and foursquare, and respectable, redolent of riverside and green fields. It was altogether appropriate that George V, the epitome of public rectitude and fair-dealing, should have been the first head of the newly named House of Windsor.

2 On the same visit to Berlin to attend the wedding of the Kaiser's only daughter, Princess Victoria Louise, to the Duke of Hanover, George V (right) – in the uniform of a German Cuirassier – poses with another cousin, the Russian Tsar Nicholas II

Chapter One
Cousins

It was with some justice that Queen Victoria was called the 'Grandmother of Europe'. In their twenty-one years of marriage she and Prince Albert produced nine children, who in turn brought thirty-nine offspring into the world. The fertility of the House of Saxe-Coburg-Gotha was to survive triumphantly – if in a more moderate way – the family's change of name to Windsor.

The international ramifications of the royal family in 1917 were impressive and, overall, sustained by a considerable warmth of feeling manifested in letter-writing, present-giving and mutual entertaining. It would be a mistake, however, to suppose that anything like a royal mafia existed, working effectively behind the scenes and circumventing the traditional channels of diplomacy. Though Queen Victoria's children and grandchildren kept family ties alive they were, in the last resort, merely the gilt on the gingerbread of power politics. No amount of correspondence between King-Emperor, Kaiser and Tsar in 1914 was able to avert a war to which the governments of the great powers, with some show of reluctance, found themselves committed. A royal visit could cap a diplomatic initiative here, or a private letter could touch upon a delicate problem there, but that was about all.

In a way, this was a pity because in 1917 the British royal family was linked by ties of blood and marriage to the German Kaiser, the Tsar of all the Russias, the King of Greece, the King of Romania, the King of Spain, the Crown Prince of Sweden, the King of Norway, the King of Denmark, the Duke of Teck, the Grand Duke of Hesse, the Duke of Saxe-Coburg-Gotha, the Duke of Schleswig-Holstein, the Duke of Brunswick and other assorted princes and noblemen. Though France obstinately remained a republic, and the Hapsburgs of Austria were outside the family circle, the majority of the crowned heads of the European powers belonged to the same family.

The two most powerful and illustrious cousins of George V were the Kaiser and the Tsar. Wilhelm II had carried out his duties as Queen Victoria's grandson with panache, genuine affection and a little melodrama. He had, however, been deeply mortified by the easy and apparently condescending bearing of his uncle King Edward VII. In these two relationships were reflected the Kaiser's love-hate relationship with Britain, emotions which were perhaps never reconciled even during his exile in the Netherlands after his abdication in 1918.

He found his diffident and unpretentious cousin King George far easier to get along with than the late King Edward, and when in 1911 the former invited him to the unveiling of Queen Victoria's memorial he replied with considerable warmth: 'You cannot imagine how overjoyed I am at the prospect of seeing you again so soon and making a nice stay with you. . . . You are perfectly right in alluding to my devotion & reverence for my beloved Grandmother. . . . Never in my life shall I forget the solemn hours in Osborne at her death-bed when she breathed her last in my arms! These sacred hours have riveted my heart firmly to your house & family, of which I am proud to feel myself a member. . . . You refer to the fact of my being her eldest grandson: a fact I was always immensely proud of and never forgot.'

Anxious though the Kaiser was on this occasion to improve Anglo-German relations, the governments of the two nations made it plain that his visit was, in their eyes, simply a family affair with no political or diplomatic implications.

The Tsar of Russia, Nicholas II, lacked the flamboyance and the sometimes aggressive verve of his cousin the Kaiser. In personality he had much more in common with George V, and in appearance the two men were so remarkably similar that when they met there were often flurries over mistaken identity. King George felt warmly towards the Tsar, telling Queen Victoria in 1894 after Nicholas's wedding to Princess Alix of Hesse (another grand-child of the old Queen): 'Nicky has been kindness itself to me, he is the same dear boy he has always been to me & talks to me quite openly on every subject.'

Neither the Kaiser nor the Tsar, however, had kept their crowns by the end of the Great War. Wilhelm II was doomed to twenty-two years of exile, but Nicholas II and his whole family were murdered by the Bolsheviks in July 1918. King George never forgot or forgave this outrage, and when Ramsay MacDonald formed the first Labour government in 1924 and the recognition of Soviet Russia was mooted, he told the new Prime Minister 'how abhorrent it would be to His Majesty to receive any representative of Russia who, directly or indirectly, had been connected with the abominable murder of the Emperor, Empress and their family, the King's own first cousin'.

Among other notable cousins of the Windsor family was Queen Marie of Romania, the daughter of Queen Victoria's second son Alfred, Duke of Edinburgh. Known to the family as 'Missy', Marie was clever, conceited and melodramatic, and her departure for Bucharest removed a restless spirit from the immediate family circle. In 1922 King George's second son the Duke of York (the future George VI) was sent to represent the House of Windsor at the marriage of Queen Marie's daughter, Princess Marie, to Alexander, King of Yugo-slavia. Queen Marie subsequently told King George V: 'Everyone much appreciated that you sent one of your sons and were awfully pleased. . . . Somehow your boy in some ways reminded me so much of you, though he has exactly May's smile, but his movements were yours and his hands.'

Queen Marie of Romania, née 'Missy' of Edinburgh, made her own contribution to the solution of the Balkan problem in the interwar years. Not only did she provide a Queen for Yugoslavia, and was herself the consort of the King of Romania, but her second daughter Elizabeth married the King of Greece, George II, while her eldest son became King Carol II of Romania in 1930.

The enviable constitutional stability of the House of Windsor was, however, denied to these far-flung cousins in the Balkans. The future King Carol II was exiled in the last years of his father's reign; yet in 1930 he returned, displaced his nine-year-old son King Michael, and was recognized as sovereign. In 1940 the Romanian dictator, Antonescu, in turn deposed King Carol and Prince Michael once more became King. After the formation of a Communist government in 1946, King Michael was forced to abdicate.

The Yugoslav branch of the family had an equally disturbed history. On 9 October

4 Queen Victoria and family group at Osborne House on the Isle of Wight, 1896. From left to right: Prince Leopold of Battenburg, Princess Aribert of Anhalt, Prince Edward (later Edward VIII), the Duchess of York (later Queen Mary), Princess Mary, Princess Margaret of Connaught, Prince Alexander of Battenburg (on ground), Prince Albert of York (later George VI), the Duke of York (later George V), Queen Victoria, Prince Arthur of Connaught, the Duchess of Connaught, Princess Patricia of Connaught (on ground), Princess Henry of Battenburg, Princess Ena of Battenburg, Princess Victoria of Schleswig-Holstein, Prince Maurice of Battenburg

5 (Below) Descendants of the previous group gather for the christening of Prince Michael of Kent in 1942. In addition to the English royal family, the group includes King Haakon of Norway, King George of the Hellenes, Prince Bernhard of the Netherlands, and the Crown Prince and Princess of Norway

1934 King Alexander I was assassinated at Marseilles during a state visit to France. His son King Peter II lost his throne when the Communists took over Yugoslavia at the end of the Second World War.

The Greek connection was a somewhat happier one constitutionally, at least until King Constantine's flight from the Colonels in 1967, though subject to some marital discord since the marriages of Princess Helen of Greece to Carol II of Romania and that of King George II to Princess Elizabeth of Romania both ended in divorce. The grandparents of George and Helen of Greece, King George I and Queen Olga, had earlier, however, earned a special place in the affections of George V. In 1882 while on a world cruise in the *Bacchante* Prince George and his elder brother, Albert Victor, had visited their Greek relatives in Athens. Prince George loved Queen Olga like a second mother and recorded in his diary a poignant account of their parting: 'We had to say goodbye to darling Aunt Olga & cousins. We all cryed, very much, we have spent such a delightful time here.'

A warm royal correspondence continued to flow between Greece and Britain as a result of these strong emotions. King George I of Greece (Uncle Willy to the family) wrote long and frequent letters to Prince George, sprinkled with affectionate descriptions like 'my dear old sausage' and 'my dear old pickled pork'. Apart from these gastronomic endearments, a new and more tangible link was forged in November 1934 when Prince George, Duke of Kent, the third son of George V, married Princess Marina of Greece.

The matrimonial fortunes of King George and Queen Mary's children provided some interesting contrasts. Although all of them married during George V's reign except Prince John (who suffered from epilepsy and died in 1919) and, of course, the Prince of Wales, only the Duke of Kent married a foreign princess. The others married home-grown aristocrats: the Duke of York celebrated his wedding to Lady Elizabeth Bowes-Lyon in 1923; Prince Henry, Duke of Gloucester, married Lady Alice Montagu-Douglas-Scott in 1935, and in 1922 Princess Mary had married Viscount Lascelles, later 6th Earl of Harewood.

The Prince of Wales, 'Dear David', did not marry during his father's lifetime, though zestful and attractive and one of the most eligible bachelors in the English-speaking world. When he did marry in 1937, after his dramatic abdication, his partner was not a princess, not an English nobleman's daughter, not even Cinderella (an appropriate enough bride for 'Prince Charming'), she was Mrs Wallis Warfield Simpson, an American and, even worse, twice divorced. As happy as this bitterly controversial marriage undoubtedly was, it produced no offspring, and as a result the House of Windsor was denied some half-American cousins of dubious 'respectability'.

If the New World was thus unable to trim the staid convention of the Old, the marriages of George V's grandchildren brought fresh blood, not all of it particularly blue, into the family. Oddly, the most exotic-sounding match, that of George VI's eldest daughter Princess Elizabeth with Prince Philip of Greece, was more in keeping with tradition. Philip was the son of Prince Andrew of Greece and Alice of Battenburg; through his mother he traced his descent from Queen Victoria's second daughter Princess Alice; his father was the son of King George I and Queen Olga of Greece (the 'Uncle Willy' and 'Aunt Olga' of George V's youth), and a nephew of Edward VII's wife Queen Alexandra. The Battenburg connection was consequently very much a family matter; more than that, Lord Louis Mountbatten, bearing the prudently anglicized version of his name, was

6 *The parents of the first head of the House of Windsor were married in March 1863. The Prince of Wales (later Edward VII) was aged twenty-one, Princess Alexandra nineteen*

a cousin, contemporary and confidant of George VI. Prince Philip had, moreover, met Princess Elizabeth as early as 1939.

In May 1960 Princess Margaret, the late King George VI's second daughter, was also married. Five years before she had reluctantly renounced her love for the divorced Group-Captain Peter Townsend after a stormy and well-publicized courtship; now she married Anthony Armstrong-Jones, a commoner and a fashionable and successful photographer: a commoner *and* a photographer! What would George V have made of that? Of course, Armstrong-Jones was not a commoner from Ebbw Vale or the dock-land of Liverpool; his father was a distinguished Q.C. and his mother the Countess of Rosse. On the other hand, he was hardly in the Windsor tradition of royal or impeccably aristocratic suitors for the female members of the house.

In 1961 the 4th Duke of Kent married Katherine Worsley, daughter of a Yorkshire baronet, whose family has held land in that county since the days of Queen Elizabeth I. Then in 1963 Princess Alexandra, daughter of the Duke of Kent who had died in a flying accident in 1942, married the Honourable Angus Ogilvie, the son of the Earl of Airlie whose family was connected with that of the Queen Mother. The two sons of George VI's sister Mary, the Princess Royal, had previously married: the 7th Earl of Harewood married Marion Stein, a concert pianist, and his brother, Gerald Lascelles, married Angela Dowding; the Earl of Harewood's marriage produced three children before it ended in divorce, that of his brother, one son. The second half of the twentieth century has thus produced a whole new crop of Windsor cousins, and, with the marriage of Princess Anne to Captain Mark Phillips (an Olympic gold medallist and a descendant of the 1st Earl of Marlborough), promises to produce some more.

7 Royal daughters of Christian IX of Denmark:
Alexandra (right) became Queen of England, Marie
became Empress of Russia, marrying Tsar Alexander III

8 (Left) Family outing at Windsor in 1907: Kaiser Wilhelm II (right) with his uncles Edward VII and the Duke of Connaught

9 (Above) Two royal families gather at Cowes in 1908: Edward VII is seated between Tsar Nicholas II of Russia and the Tsarina

10 (Below) After the war and the Russian revolution: the Dowager Empress of Russia (in black cloak), in the company of her sister Queen Alexandra, George V – first head of the House of Windsor – and Queen Mary, attends the wedding of the Duke of Beaufort in 1923

11 Honours were readily available to the family. In 1911 the Order of the Garter was given to Edward, the young Prince of Wales (on right), King Manuel of Portugal (left) and the Duke of Connaught

12 Queen Alexandra and Prince Olaf of Norway board the royal yacht at Calais, 1912

13 The Duke of York (later George VI) rides with the Crown Prince of Serbia in London in 1916

14 (Below) King Boris of Bulgaria at Balmoral in 1927 with George V and the Duke of York

15 *Balkan cousins at a christening in 1923: Queen Marie of Romania (daughter of Queen Victoria's second son, Alfred, Duke of Edinburgh) holds her grandson, the Crowned Prince of Yugoslavia. She is attended (l to r) by King Alexander of Yugoslavia, her daughter Elizabeth (Queen of Greece), her husband King Ferdinand of Romania, and the Duke and Duchess of York*

16 *Princess Marie Louise, grand-daughter of Queen Victoria, and her elder sister with their father Prince Christian of Schleswig-Holstein in 1879*

17 *Princess Marie Louise in old age with Lord Wavell at a meeting of Boer War Nursing Sisters, seventy years later*

18 *(Below) Norwegian cousins: Queen Elizabeth and the Duke of Edinburgh with (from left, standing) Princess Astrid, Prince Harald, Princess Ragnhild fru Lorentzen, and (sitting) King Haakon VII and Crown Prince Olav, in 1955*

19–22 At home in England the family ties have always been close

23 The bond between Lord Louis Mountbatten and his cousins has been particularly notable. In 1919 Edward, Prince of Wales, took time off from his world tour to indulge in a little horseplay with Mountbatten (at back)

24 (Below) In 1933 the Duke of York presented a golf cup to Louis Mountbatten at Ranelagh

25 In 1922 Princess Mary married Viscount Lascelles
(later 6th Earl of Harewood), and a whole new group of
cousins was to emerge

26 Princess Alexandra, daughter of the Duke of Kent, married the Hon. Angus Ogilvie in 1963, five years before this photograph was taken

27 In 1964 Prince Charles (right) and Prince Michael of Kent maintained the links with the Greek royal family by attending the wedding of King Constantine of Greece and Princess Anne-Marie of Denmark

28 (Below right) Three years later the King and Queen of Greece finally abandoned their country to the Colonels and flew to exile in Rome

29 (Left) Princess Marina of Greece had married into the House of Windsor in 1934, when she became Duchess of Kent

30 Shortly before her wedding, she was painted by the pre-eminent portrait artist of the period, Philip de Lazlo. Jarché, who took this photograph, had crept into the room unobserved

31 (Below) The Duke and Duchess of Kent on honeymoon in Salzburg

32 In 1941 the Duchess of Kent's father, King George of Greece, reached England – a refugee from fascism

34 Prince Philip aged nine, in Greek national costume. He signed the photograph himself

33 The most famous Greek arrival in the House of Windsor was, of course, Prince Philip. In 1947 – the year of his marriage to Princess Elizabeth – he is shown (as Lieutenant Philip Mountbatten) with his three sisters, all born Princesses of Greece

35 *The bearded face of the naval officer: Prince Philip in 1945 was serving with the Royal Navy as second-in-command of a destroyer in the Pacific Fleet*

36 *It was widely thought that Princess Margaret would marry the divorced Group-Captain Peter Townsend, and thus emulate her uncle Edward VIII, who had abdicated in order to marry the American divorcee, Mrs Simpson. Townsend flew her plane 'The Last of the Many' in the King's Cup air race in 1950*

37 *(Below) Instead, ten years later, she married Anthony Armstrong-Jones, a commoner and a photographer*

38 *(Right) In 1968 the sharply dressed Earl of Snowdon left for Barbados in the company of his wife and three-year-old daughter, Lady Sarah Armstrong-Jones*

39 The most recent Windsor engagement was announced in June 1973. Princess Anne and Lieutenant Mark Phillips, an Olympic Gold Medallist, were brought together by their fondness for horses

0 *Together at the Chatsworth horse trials in October
972*

*1 (Below left) At Chatsworth Lt. Phillips came first,
Princess Anne second*

42 *(Below right) Speculation over Prince Charles's
marital prospects continued. Here he is seen with an
'anonymous' girl-friend after a visit to the theatre in 1967*

Chapter Two

Court Circular

The British constitution is, arguably, a republic heavily disguised as a monarchy. It is part of the benign pretence that the births, marriages, anniversaries and deaths of monarchs and their families are celebrated with due pomp and ceremony. There is little good copy for the press in lavish paeons in celebration of the Prime Minister's birthday; television's TAM ratings are not going to be boosted by a lengthy coverage of the Silver Wedding of the Minister for the Environment. But the marital and gynaecological functions of the House of Windsor are a different matter, and even the steady accumulation of years can provoke a rapturous acclaim denied to old-age pensioners in Glasgow or Hackney Wick.

Births are normally appropriate for celebration. But the future King George VI chose to enter the world on 14 December 1895, the fateful anniversary of the death of his long and deeply-mourned grandfather Prince Albert. Alarmed lest Queen Victoria react unfavourably to this tactlessly-timed arrival, the baby's father, Prince George, wrote to his grandmother asking her to act as godmother and also announcing his intention to name the child Albert. Queen Victoria responded very sensibly saying: 'Most gladly do I accept being Godmother to this dear little boy, born on the day his beloved Great Grandfather entered on an even greater life. He will be specially dear to me.'

With Queen Victoria's death in 1901, a good deal of the gloom surrounding 14 December vanished; so too did the need to struggle with her over the choice of names for royal infants. Not that everything was plain sailing in this respect. King George V had approved wholeheartedly of 'Elizabeth, Alexandra, Mary' for the 'little darling with a lovely complexion & pretty fair hair' who was born to the Duke and Duchess of York (the future King George VI and Queen Elizabeth) on 21 April 1926. But four years later when a second daughter was born on 13 August 1930 at Glamis, the Duchess of York's ancestral home, King George objected to Ann as a first name, and the baby's mother later resignedly wrote to Queen Mary that 'Bertie and I have decided now to call our little daughter Margaret Rose . . . as Papa does not like Ann – I hope that you like it'.

By 1950, however, George V had been dead for fourteen years and the prejudice against 'Ann' had died with him; there was now no reason why the second child of Princess Elizabeth and Prince Philip should not be named 'Anne'. The christening of her brother 'Charles, Philip, Arthur, George' on 15 December 1948 similarly aroused no family controversy even though it reinstated a first name with strong connections with the not altogether happy house of Stuart.

One remarkable custom connected with royal births was scrapped after Princess Margaret was born in 1930. During James II's reign (1685–8) there had been fears of a plot to kidnap the baby male heir at his birth; ever since, a minister of the crown had been in attendance

43 The death of Edward VII is announced to the crowd
by a notice on the railings of Buckingham Palace in 1910.
The reign of the House of Windsor is about to begin in
practice, although the name of 'Windsor' was not adopted
until 1917

39

at royal confinements to thwart similar dastardly plans. On 5 August 1930 the Labour Home Secretary, J. R. Clynes, an ex-mill hand, had sped post-haste to Glamis; his arrival was premature, that of the baby princess was not, and one of the leading ministers of Ramsay MacDonald's government was kept hanging about until 21 August. When Prince Charles was born in November 1948, the Home Secretary was merely informed of the fact by telephone.

Royal christenings in Britain are straightforward, almost austere, affairs compared with some of the rituals that have surrounded similar events among the Windsor cousins on the continent. In 1923, for example, the Duke of York (the future George VI) was invited to Belgrade to stand as 'Koom' (Godfather) to the infant son of King Alexander of Yugoslavia. On 21 October the ceremonies began, and the Duke of York, who was, in any event, of a shy and retiring disposition, was obliged to receive a set of hand-embroidered underwear from the child's parents. He also had entire charge of the baby during the rituals. This was just as well, for the aged Patriarch, on receiving the Crown Prince for baptism, dropped him in the font, whence he was scooped up by his alert 'Koom'. The Duke of York later wrote to his father: 'You can imagine what I felt like carrying the baby on a cushion. It screamed most of the time which drowned the singing & the service altogether.'

It was not, however, desirable to drag members of the Windsor family screaming to the altar. Their choice of marriage partner, though subject to certain restrictions, was made as free as possible. Not that all acquired their brides and grooms in a whirlwind of romantic and tempestuous ardour; indeed Edward VIII, who did just that, paid for it with his crown. His father George V, on the other hand, married Princess Mary (May) of Teck only after her engagement to his elder brother, the backward and listless Albert Victor, Duke of Clarence, had been cut short by the latter's sudden death in 1892. At first, Prince George and Princess May made a stiff and awkward couple; but their relationship blossomed, and some months after their wedding Prince George wrote with his habitual candour: '... when I asked you to marry me, I was very fond of you, but not very much in love with you ... I have tried to understand you & to know you, & with the happy result that I know now that I do *love* you darling girl with all my heart, & am simply *devoted* to you ... I *adore you sweet May*.'

George V's surviving children, with the exception of the future Edward VIII, chose their partners in a more congenial atmosphere. On 28 February 1922 Princess Mary married Lord Lascelles, and her father recorded in his diary a not unusual paternal reaction: 'I went up to Mary's room and took leave of her & quite broke down. . . . Felt very down and depressed now that darling Mary has gone.' When a year later the King's second son, the Duke of York, married Lady Elizabeth Bowes-Lyon in Westminster Abbey, he wrote to the bridegroom: 'You are indeed a lucky man to have such a charming and delightful wife as Elizabeth. . . . I trust that you both will have many years of happiness before you & that you will be as happy as Mama & I am after you have been married for 30 years. I can't wish you more.'

In 1947 King George VI saw his own daughter Elizabeth married to Prince Philip. The two cousins had corresponded throughout the war, and Princess Elizabeth had apparently fallen in love with the young naval cadet at their first meeting in 1939. But King George was not keen on an early engagement, telling his mother, Queen Mary, in 1944: 'We

40

44 *George V, who came to the throne in 1910, married Princess May of Teck in 1893*

45 *(Overleaf) George V's coronation procession, 1911*

46 Peers leaving Westminster Abbey after the coronation of George V

47 Edward VIII, although King, was never crowned. The next coronation (shown here) was that of George VI in 1937

both think she is too young for that now, as she has never met any young men of her own age.' He added, however: 'I like Philip. He is intelligent, and has a good sense of humour & thinks about things in the right way.'

Three years later on 20 November 1947 'Lilibet' married Prince Philip, now a British subject, in Westminster Abbey. Although the marriage service was, in the words of the Archbishop of York, 'in all essentials exactly the same as it would be for any cottager who might be married this afternoon in some small country church in a remote village in the dales', the trappings were very different. The celebrations brought a splash of gorgeous ceremonial into the drab years of domestic austerity. As well as other Heads of State, Kings, Queens and Princes met in one of the largest and most splendid gatherings of royalty since the beginning of the century. To be sure, not all of the monarchs had thrones to sit on – but they came all the same. The service was shown on television and broadcast to the four corners of the globe. Considering that a Labour government held office with a huge majority, this royal jamboree, relying so heavily upon religious and civic tradition, provided outstanding proof of the stability of the British constitution and the important national role of the House of Windsor.

George VI later wrote a touching letter to Princess Elizabeth while she was on honeymoon:

'I was so proud of you & thrilled at having you so close to me on our long walk in Westminster Abbey, but when I handed your hand to the Archbishop I felt that I had lost something very precious. . . . I am so glad you wrote and told Mummy that you think the long wait before your engagement & the long time before the wedding was for the best. I was rather afraid that you had thought I was being hard hearted about it. . . . Your leaving us has left a great blank in our lives but do remember that your old home is still yours & do come back to it as much as possible. I can see that you are sublimely happy with Philip which is right but don't forget us is the wish of
Your ever loving and devoted
PAPA.'

Coronations provide as much opportunity for joyous celebration as royal weddings – though naturally they are far less frequent. In fact the House of Windsor has seen only two coronations since 1917, Edward VIII having abdicated before he could be crowned. King George VI approached his coronation in May 1937 with some apprehension. There were several reasons for this: six months before he had suddenly been called to take up a position for which his elder brother had been groomed all his life – he himself admitted that 'I've never seen a State Paper. I'm only a Naval Officer, it's the only thing I know about'; also, King George suffered from a speech impediment, which he had made great efforts to overcome but which still haunted him and might well be exacerbated by the strain of the coronation service and oath-taking.

When his coronation day dawned, therefore, George VI felt no uplifting of his heart, and, indeed, later recorded: 'I could eat no breakfast and had a sinking feeling inside.' Although a century had passed since an elderly peer had tumbled down the stairs at Queen Victoria's coronation, George VI underwent a series of misfortunes at his own. When the great moment came to take the Coronation Oath neither the Bishop of Durham nor Bath and Wells 'could find the words, so the Archbishop held his book down for me to read, but horror of horrors his thumb covered the words of the Oath. My Lord Great Chamberlain was supposed to dress me but I found his hands fumbled and shook so I had to fix the belt of the sword myself. . . . I never did know whether [the crown] was [on] right or not. . . . As I turned after leaving the Coronation Chair I was brought up all standing, owing to one of the Bishops treading on my robe. I had to tell him to get off it pretty sharply as I nearly fell down.'

Despite these ceremonial lapses, the coronation celebrations of 1937 were tumultuous, as if the public had once more recovered its breath after the traumas of the abdication crisis; it was also the last occasion on which a full-scale Imperial tribute was paid to the new King-Emperor.

Queen Elizabeth's coronation day on 2 June 1953 seems to have been free of serious ecclesiastic fumbling and untoward incident, even though subjected to the ruthless eye of the television camera. The main impression was of the dignity and sincerity of the new monarch in her shimmering dress and her rich coronation robe; the symbolic climax came with the placing of the crown, the St Edward's crown which weighs all of seven pounds, upon the head of the fourth monarch of the House of Windsor.

The passing of Kings, Queens and Consorts is similarly marked by particular ceremonial: flags at half-mast, the lying in state, funeral corteges, sombrely-dressed foreign dignitaries, slow marches through the streets, and slow music on radio and television. Since 1917 the Windsor family has mourned the deaths of three Kings, George V in 1936, George VI in 1952 and Edward VIII in 1972, and two Consorts, Queen Alexandra (the widow of Edward VII) in 1925, and the indomitable Queen Mary in March 1953 – only three months before her granddaughter's coronation. Yet even as the death of one monarch is announced, the accession of another is proclaimed in the same breath, and the cry 'The King is dead – Long live the Queen' reflects, at least in modern times, the inexorable continuity of the succession.

48 The coronation group, 1937. Already the memory of the abdication crisis was fading

49 The balcony at Buckingham Palace on Coronation Day, 12 May 1937. Princess Elizabeth stands between her mother and her grandmother

50 Fifteen years later, on the death of her father George VI, Elizabeth was proclaimed Queen. For the proclamation at St James's Palace the full panoply of medieval heraldry was necessary. In the centre of the group is the Earl Marshal, the Duke of Norfolk

52 *The Queen's accession to the throne was proclaimed at four historic points in London: at the Royal Exchange the task fell to the Clarenceux King of Arms. The procession had started from St James's Palace and then stopped at Charles I's statue in Charing Cross and at Temple Bar*

53 Queen Elizabeth was crowned in Westminster Abbey on 2 June 1953, clad in a white virginal dress. She waits for the moment of the Anointing

54 The crowning is over. With the Sceptre in her right hand and the Rod in her left, the Queen waits for the Archbishop of Canterbury and the senior peers to pay homage

55 (Overleaf) Clutching the symbols of Majesty, Queen
Elizabeth II, wearing the Imperial Crown, leaves
Westminster Abbey

*56 A firework display by the Fleet at Spithead follows the
Queen's inspection on 15 June 1953*

57 (Left) Successful marriages are all-important to the maintenance of the dynasty. No Windsor marriage has been more successful than that of George VI (then Duke of York) to Lady Elizabeth Bowes-Lyon, which took place on 26 April 1923

58 In 1948 they celebrated their Silver Wedding Anniversary in Westminster Abbey

59 (Overleaf left) In 1937, at a necessarily much less formal affair, ex-King Edward (now Duke of Windsor) married the American divorcee, Mrs Wallis Simpson, in France. For her, he had sacrificed the throne

60 (Overleaf right) Ten years later, an altogether happier public occasion, with a radiant bride and a resolute groom. For them the future was bright

61–4 A flashback to childhood: Princess Elizabeth, aged two, drives with her nanny in Piccadilly and, aged ten, comforts a royal corgi; Prince Philip airs his toes at the age of thirteen months and demonstrates his seamanship on the school boat some years later

65 and 66 *New roles for the royals: Prince Philip as one of the Three Wise Kings lays his crown before the cradle in a Gordonstoun School nativity play (1938); Princess Elizabeth stars in the Windsor pantomime, Christmas 1944*

67–74 The courting of Princess Elizabeth: a newsreel sequence shows Prince Philip helping the ladies disrobe at a wedding in Kent in October 1946

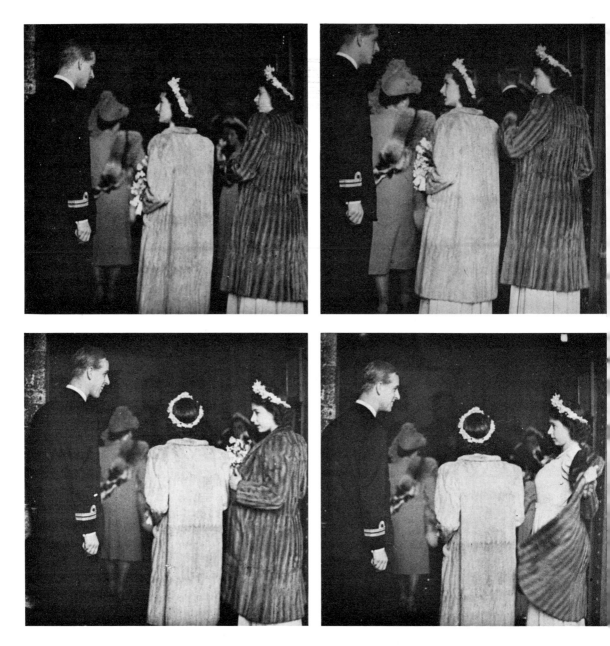

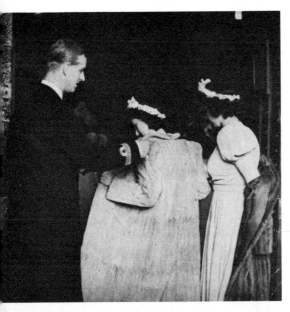 

75 *The engagement: American naval officers congratulate Princess Elizabeth and Lieutenant Philip Mountbatten during a garden party at Buckingham Palace, July 1947*

77 (Left) The photographer commented: 'The Princess has never been so easy to photograph'

78 Princess Elizabeth and the newly created Duke of Edinburgh depart in a petal-strewn carriage for Waterloo Station and their honeymoon at Broadlands, the house of the Mountbattens near Romsey in Hampshire and once the home of Lord Palmerston (20 November 1947)

79 At Broadlands: Elizabeth looks dependent and vulnerable as she has rarely done since

80 *Royal births are national events. Prince Charles was born on 14 November 1948, and this was the first picture taken of the family together (April 1949)*   81 *Princess Anne (born 15 August 1950) attempts to crawl out of the picture in Clarence House garden*

72 *Back to school: the two young Princes, Andrew (left) and Edward, return to London from Sandringham at the end of the Christmas holiday (January 1973), dragged along by royal corgis*

84 *Further royal weddings: Princess Mary, the Prince of Wales, the Duke of York and Prince George (later Duke of Kent) attend the marriage of Lord Louis Mountbatten and Lady Edwina Ashley (1924)*

85 *In 1935 the Duke and Duchess of Gloucester were married*

86   *The Court Circular would also record the complex and varied round of ceremonies. In 1913 George V and Queen Mary walked in the Garter Procession at Windsor Castle*

87   *The opening of buildings and the laying of foundation stones occupies a great amount of royal time. In 1922 George V opened the new County Hall at Westminster*

88   *(Below) In 1937 George VI and Queen Elizabeth reviewed the Fleet before boarding the royal yacht 'Victoria and Albert'*

89 In 1938 the two Princesses had a foretaste of official duties when they saw their mother launch the liner Queen Elizabeth at Glasgow

91 (Below right) Princess Elizabeth on Winston at the Trooping the Colour ceremony, 1949. Her horsemanship is invaluable on such occasions

90 (Below left) The King and Queen inspect progress on the Festival of Britain site on the South Bank in 1950

92 In 1953 the Queen presented the Colour to the Grenadiers at Windsor Castle

94 *The only serious threat in this century to the even pattern of the public life of the House of Windsor was Edward VIII's romance with Mrs Simpson. Three months before the news was published, he was photographed in a nightclub with her*

95 Barely a year later he drove into exile after his renunciation speech

96 (Below left) The Duke and Duchess of Windsor share a joke from the Duke's autobiography, A King's Story. They found a contentment together that lasted a lifetime

97 October 1945: the Duke of Windsor and his mother meet for the first time in nine years. She never really accepted the situation – or the Duchess

98–100 *Queen Elizabeth's reign began in high drama. Her father, looking strained and haggard, said goodbye to his daughter for the last time at London Airport as she left for Kenya on the first stage of her Commonwealth tour late in January 1952. Barely had she arrived in Nairobi (where a reception was held in the grounds of Government House) when the news came through that the King had died in his sleep*

101–3 *The new Queen flew immediately back to London, to be greeted by her ministers, including (right to left) Churchill, Attlee and Eden, and Lord Mountbatten, before driving with the Duke of Edinburgh to Clarence House in the evening*

104–8 The health of Kings is a matter for urgent public concern, and their deaths have been occasions of national mourning. (Left) A newspaper poster announces the death of George V. (Below) Bulletins posted on the railings of Buckingham Palace report the progress of George VI after an operation on his lungs, and an announcement at Marlborough House presages the death of Queen Mary. (Below right) 'The King is dead, long live the Queen!': the coronation invitation, June 1953

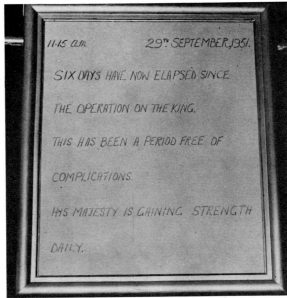

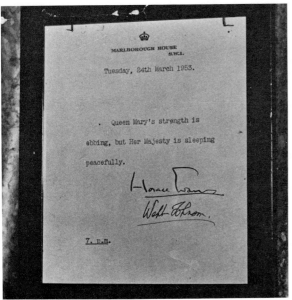

109 The deaths of monarchs receive almost as much attention as their crowning. In 1925 Edward (Prince of Wales), George V, and other royal and non-royal mourners walk in procession at the funeral of Queen Alexandra

*110 When George V died in 1936 there were four royal
sons to follow the coffin from the church at
Sandringham*

111 *The new King, Edward VIII, walks ahead of his three brothers as the funeral procession moves through the streets of London*

112 *The four sons of George V stand guard at the lying-in-state in Westminster Hall*

113 *When George VI died in 1952 the impact was cathartic. Enormous queues formed for the lying-in-state and stretched along the north bank of the Thames, over Lambeth Bridge and along the embankment on the south side, where it doubled back and wound in front of Lambeth Palace itself (far right)*

114 *(Below left) The track men at Paddington Station stand with bared heads as the train carrying the dead King leaves for Windsor*

115 (Below right) At Windsor the gun-carriage bearing the coffin passes the statue of Queen Victoria

116 (Overleaf) On the day of the funeral everything stopped for two minutes of silent homage. Even the traffic in Piccadilly was still

Chapter Three
Meet the People

One of the main functions of a constitutional monarch is to be *seen*. The monarchy embodies the work-a-day and sometimes drab apparatus of the state; it is in the sovereign's name that aircraft carriers sail, the loyal Parliamentary Opposition complains, the courts of criminal justice prosecute, and the Secretary of State for Education builds new schools. The leading members of the House of Windsor are subsequently engaged in an almost ceaseless round of official duties, from the State Opening of Parliament to the planting of inaugural cherry trees in obscure corners of the provinces. In this way, the sovereign, the well-regarded personification of the State, actually meets the people.

Not that all members of the royal family necessarily revel in the limelight. After the death of the Prince Consort in 1861, Queen Victoria, who was shy at the best of times, turned herself into a mourning recluse; even though her son, the future Edward VII, positively sought out the public gaze and was even involved in some unsavoury scandals, the withdrawal of the Queen led to a decade of rising republican sentiment.

Although King Edward VII was by no means of a retiring disposition, his son was. As a young man King George V had been remarkably sensitive to criticism, which was almost certainly a reflection of a fundamental lack of confidence; even the irascibility and dog-matism which marked his later years may have stemmed from these former insecurities. His first attempts at public speechmaking cost him a great deal in nervous tension, though after 1893 the steady support of his wife, Princess Mary, was a tremendous help. Eventually George V developed an unusual rapport with his people which was based to a very large degree upon his kindly and straightforward bearing in public.

George VI, like his father, was originally destined for a steady advancement in the Royal Navy. Though sensible and courageous, he had, from the cradle, suffered from a series of gastric disorders that were, at least in part, the reflection of acute nervousness; he also stammered. His anxieties on the latter score were greatly heightened by his accession and the new and pressing public demands that this entailed. His speech impediment had been referred to in a broadcast delivered by the Archbishop of Canterbury, Dr Lang, in December 1936. Dr Lang said of the new King: 'When his people listen to him they will note an occasional and momentary hesitation in his speech. But he has brought it into full control, and to those who hear it need cause no sort of embarrassment, for it causes none to him who speaks.'

This brisk episcopal explanation was, unfortunately, quite inaccurate in two respects: King George had not brought his stammer under *full* control, otherwise it would not have posed a problem; moreover, his speech impediment caused him agonies of embarrassment, at least in his early days as monarch, though the anticipation of speechmaking was often

92

117 In an age of rapid transport the task of showing the Royal Presence to the people was immensely simplified. George V and Queen Mary drive in the royal limousine in 1934

worse than the event. His long and determined struggle to master his stammer was eventually rewarded with remarkable success. Still, it did not make his public appearances, especially those involving speechmaking, any easier to bear.

In contrast, other members of the House of Windsor have positively thrived on public contact. As Prince of Wales, Edward VIII was an indefatigable and matchless public relations man for the monarchy. Of course, he had his blind spots, finding the annual presentation of debutantes boring and his dutiful partnering of dull wives at official dances irksome. In other respects he was the sparkling mirror of the 1920s and early thirties: fashionably dressed, piloting his own plane, in touch with the phenomena of the 'flapper' era, and apparently concerned with contemporary problems.

After 1947 the monarchy acquired a recruit of similar zest and with an equivalent flair for public contact when Prince Philip married Princess Elizabeth. Prince Philip's easy and self-confident manner, though spiced with an intolerance of official humbug, has proved well-suited to an increasingly democratic age. There is no doubt that the performance of the Queen's public duties has benefited from the relaxed deportment of her Consort.

In what ways, however, does the monarch actually meet the people? Each year there are a number of 'hardy annuals': about a dozen investitures, Maundy Thursday, the Queen's Scout Parade at Windsor on Easter Sunday, the F.A. Cup Final, the Trooping of the Colour (the Queen's Official Birthday Parade), the Derby at Epsom, Royal Ascot, Installations of the Orders of the Garter and the Thistle, various Garden Parties, Goodwood, the Braemar Gathering, the State Opening of Parliament, the Remembrance Day Service at the Cenotaph, the Diplomatic Presentation Party, the Christmas Day broadcast. In addition, the monarch nowadays will mostly attend the Royal Variety Performance and the Royal Film Performance, some public exhibitions (like the Ideal Home Exhibition), the Second Test Match at Lord's, an international rugby match at Twickenham, some sessions during Wimbledon fortnight, the Badminton Horse Trials and other equestrian events.

Then there are the regional tours. These were begun in 1912 when George V and Queen Mary visited South Wales and the West Riding of Yorkshire, and the King became the first British sovereign to go down a coal mine – as well as being privileged to overhear his subjects' frank, and not always complimentary, opinions of him. Since then regional tours have claimed an increasingly large part of the monarch's annual duties. The tours normally last for two or three days and involve the royal party in an arduous round of hand-shaking, small talk, sight-seeing, interest-taking (real or feigned), smiling and waving. An American Presidential candidate on the stump can hardly have a more exacting programme, and, unlike him, the monarch cannot even indulge in the catharsis of angry speeches directed at malevolent political foes – for the royal house in its domestic context has, in theory, no foes to attack.

Although the royal visitors are whisked to Aberdeen or Barnstaple or Widnes in especially appointed trains, cars, or aeroplanes, the plush interior of the Queen's day coach on the royal train or the noiseless progress of a Rolls Royce saloon can hardly compensate for the intervening hours packed with vigilance and strung together with smiles – for the public virtually demands that its constitutional monarch should, where appropriate, appear wreathed in smiles.

The fearsome pressures of a typical regional tour are clearly shown in the records of the

118 In 1911 George V and Queen Mary presented the young Prince of Wales to the Welsh people after the Investiture at Caernarvon Castle (a ceremony revived after 600 years of disuse)

19–20 In 1969 – a space age away from the previous occasion – Queen Elizabeth presents Prince Charles to the Welsh people, despite the persistent rumbles of Welsh nationalism

Court Circular. Here is the itinerary of *one day* in the royal tour of Lincolnshire in June 1958:

'The Queen and the Duke of Edinburgh arrived at LINCOLN this morning and were received by the Earl of Ancaster (Her Majesty's Lieutenant for Lincolnshire), Sir Denis Le Marchant (High Sheriff) and the Mayor (Councillor L. H. Priestley), who presented to The Queen the King Richard II Sword which Her Majesty was pleased to return.

'Her Majesty and His Royal Highness drove to the USHER ART GALLERY where presentations were made. The Queen and the Duke of Edinburgh then drove to the LINCOLN CITY FOOTBALL GROUND where the school children were assembled.

'Her Majesty and His Royal Highness subsequently drove to the PELHAM BRIDGE where The Queen unveiled a commemorative tablet and declared the Bridge open.

'Her Majesty and the Duke of Edinburgh then drove to the CATHEDRAL and were received by the Bishop of Lincoln (the Right Reverend Kenneth Riches, D.D.) and the Dean of Lincoln (the Right Reverend Colin Dunlop). Her Majesty, with His Royal Highness, toured the CATHEDRAL and unveiled a Window in the Airmen's Chapel.

'In the Chapter House The Queen sat in the chair occupied by King Edward I when he opened Parliament in Lincoln in 1301. The Queen and the Duke of Edinburgh then visited the CASTLE and subsequently left Lincoln in the Royal Train for SCUNTHORPE. Upon arrival at SCUNTHORPE this afternoon Her Majesty and His Royal Highness were received by the Mayor (Councillor Mrs Violet Wilmshurst).

'The Queen and the Duke of Edinburgh drove to the CIVIC THEATRE and visited the OLD PEOPLE'S RECREATIONAL CENTRE. (They spoke to many old people, and planted trees in THE FESTIVAL GARDENS.)

'Her Majesty opened the new MODEL TRAFFIC AREA and later, with His Royal Highness, drove to the TECHNICAL COLLEGE.

'The Queen and the Duke of Edinburgh were received by Sir Weston Cracrofts-Amcotts (Chairman of the County Council) and toured the COLLEGE.

'Her Majesty and His Royal Highness subsequently drove to the APPELBY-FRODING-HAM STEEL WORKS and were received by Sir Walter Benton-Jones (the Chairman).

'The Queen and the Duke of Edinburgh toured the WORKS and proceeded to the ROYAL LAWN where presentations were made.

'Her Majesty and His Royal Highness then drove to the REDBOURN WORKS of Messrs Richard Thomas and Baldwins Limited and proceeded to IMMINGHAM DOCKS.

'The Queen and the Duke of Edinburgh were received by General Sir Brian Robertson, Bt. (Chairman, British Transport Commission), and embarked in H.M. YACHT "BRITANNIA".

'The Countess of Euston, Sir Edward Ford, Captain the Lord Plunket and Mr Esmond Butler were in attendance.

'The Queen and the Duke of Edinburgh gave a dinner party on board the ROYAL YACHT this evening. The following had the honour of being invited:

The Earl of Ancaster, the Earl and Countess of Yarborough, the Viscount Crookshank, the Bishop of Lincoln and Mrs Riches, and Wing Commander and Mrs Beresford Horsley.'

It is also considered appropriate that the House of Windsor should show its concern for public tragedies. For global disasters, earthquakes, famines, floods and the like, a carefully-drafted message of sympathy is the practical limit of royal involvement. But for domestic catastrophes a personal visit is both possible and expedient. During the first regional tour in 1912 King George and Queen Mary were able to visit Cadeby Pit in the West Riding where seventy-eight miners had died the day before. In 1968 the Queen's grief was evident when she visited the desolate scene of the Aberfan disaster.

The real effect of monarchical visitations of this sort is naturally open to question; mutual regard apparently flourishes amid the ruins and bereavement occasioned by disasters; whether this alone transforms Trotskyists into royalists or turns princes into egalitarians is a matter for doubt. Edward VIII, when Prince of Wales, had some sharp criticisms of workers' living conditions; there is little evidence that any substantial improvement resulted from these royal strictures. King George V and Queen Mary, though privately giving money to alleviate the effects of unemployment, often failed to equate strike action with genuine grievances and generally considered the prospect of industrial conflict as a tiresome interruption in the life of the nation. Nonetheless the House of Windsor has consistently shown that Britain's constitutional monarchy has a very human face, and this has undoubtedly contributed something to national unity.

Apart from the annual routine of meeting the people, there have also been a number of special, quasi-formal, occasions for contact. Twice since 1910 a Prince of Wales has been presented to the Welsh nation: in 1911 and again in 1969. The ceremony at Caernarvon in 1911 owed a great deal to the inspired improvisation of the Liberal Chancellor of the Exchequer, David Lloyd George, since it was more than 600 years since Edward I had presented his son to the Welsh as their prince. Lloyd George even taught the future King Edward VIII to say, in Welsh, "All Wales is a Sea of Song' and 'Thanks from the bottom of my heart to the old land of my fathers'. This was no small achievement for a prince through whose veins flowed predominantly the blood of the House of Hanover and Saxe-Coburg-Gotha.

In 1969 Prince Charles went through a similar investiture with considerable poise and dignity, despite earlier Welsh nationalist agitation that included the explosion of a few home-made bombs. The ceremony itself is fundamentally a rootless hotch-potch, though pleasing to the eye. At least in 1969 the poet Robert Graves wrote a verse which linked Prince Charles in direct line of descent to the sixth-century Pendragon:

> *Thrice fortunate is he who winneth*
> *As heir to Maelgwyn Pendragon*
> *Grand welcome at the heart of Gwynedd:*
> *Setting his princely feet upon*
> *Those golden streets of Sinadon*
> *And guarded against evil will*
> *By Dewi Sant's own daffodil.*

Silver Weddings provide further occasional opportunities to join with the people in celebration. In July 1918 King George V and Queen Mary, conscious of the restraint necessary in wartime, marked their twenty-fifth wedding anniversary with quiet dignity. On 26 April 1948 King George VI and Queen Elizabeth celebrated their Silver Wedding Day with a service at St Paul's Cathedral and a modest progress through the streets of

London. 'We were both dumbfounded over our reception,' King George later wrote with pleasure to his mother. In 1972 it was the turn of King George's daughter, Queen Elizabeth II, to celebrate the twenty-fifth anniversary of her marriage to Prince Philip, the Duke of Edinburgh.

The House of Windsor can boast only one Silver Jubilee to date – and then only just, for King George V died nine months after the Jubilee of May 1935. The public response to the King's twenty-five years on the throne was a warm, spontaneous outpouring of affection that surprised and mystified many observers; the citizens of the backstreets of London were as rapturous as the inhabitants of middle-class boroughs, and Queen Mary noted that 'the decorations in the smaller streets . . . were very touching, many people recognized us and cheered'. King George was deeply moved by his reception and remarked candidly: 'I'd no idea they felt like that about me. I am beginning to think they must like me for myself.' The feeling of mutual respect and affection thus manifested in 1935 could indeed serve as a model for the harmony that is so desirable between a constitutional monarch and his people.

121 George V and Queen Mary appeared at most times to be stiff and formal, yet their unbending devotion to duty won them the respect and, finally, the affection of the people

122 *Edward VIII whilst Prince of Wales won enormous popularity with his charm and informal elegance – in striking contrast to the more ponderous style of his father. Here, together with his brother Albert, later George VI (behind), he pays a visit to the City in 1919*

123 *The Prince of Wales is the centre of attention at a Chelsea football match in the same year*

124 *As King, Edward continued to favour more informal attitudes. Here he goes on 'walkabout' in London*

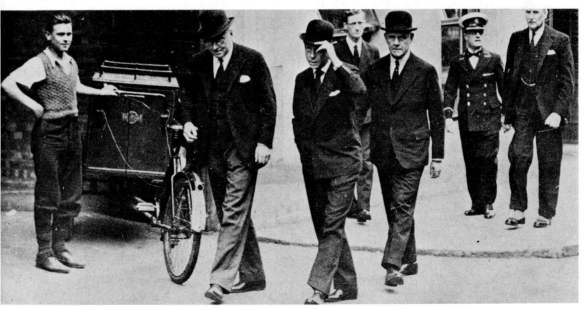

125 *One of Edward's most famous visits was to the unemployed in South Wales. It was here that he demanded: 'Something must be done'*

126 *Whilst Edward seemed to be taking the House of Windsor firmly into the twentieth century, other members did not find the transition quite so easy – although the Duke of York, fired by his elder brother's example, branched out into other activities, such as driving a Glasgow tram in 1924*

127 (Left) Queen Mary was usually very conscious of her dignity – though when she smiled, as at the centenary celebrations of University College, London, in 1927, she melted many hearts

128 George V doffs the royal topper at the opening of Canada House in Trafalgar Square, 1925

129 *Visits to coalmines were to become quite popular. In*
1912 Queen Mary visited Silverwood Colliery in
Yorkshire, and George V – who was with her – became the
first British sovereign to go down a coalmine

130 *The Prince of Wales equally favoured the idea*

131 Queen Mary visiting allotment holders at Datchet in 1919

132 In Hyde Park during the great Peace celebrations of 1919

133 (Below) Queen Mary in 1937 at a children's garden party in Lambeth Palace. Her companion, the Archbishop of Canterbury Dr Cosmo Lang, had recently disapproved of her eldest son's activities

134 (Left) Well-publicized attendance at popular events was an obvious way of meeting the people. At the Wembley Exhibition in 1925 the King and Queen rode on a miniature Canadian Pacific Railway

135 The famous French tennis star, Suzanne Lenglen, was received by Queen Mary at Wimbledon in 1926

136 Queen Mary visited Southwark in 1947 on an obviously informal occasion

137 (Below) The marriage of the Duchess of Kent brought a new style and a more modern look to royal visits. In 1937 the Duke and Duchess were at a garden party with Noel Coward

138 *Sunderland for the Cup, 1937*

139 *(Below left) The Duke of York at a boys' camp in New Romney, Hampshire: always conscious of the 'two nations', he hoped that such camps would encourage boys of all classes to mix*

140 *(Below right) As King, he continued to show an active interest in this field. Here he joins in the 'chestnut tree' song at Southwold boys' camp in Suffolk*

141 *(Right) Crowds surge round the royal car on a visit to the East End in 1937*

142 *(Overleaf) In the same year the new King and Queen with their daughters, attended a ceremony of the Royal Company of Archers at Holyrood Palace*

143 (Left) George VI had a very acute sense of occasion
but more sense of humour than his father. In 1929 he wore
the full dress of the Cameron Highlanders after receiving
the key to Edinburgh

144 Opening the National Maritime Museum at
Greenwich in 1937

145 *Most members of the House of Windsor appear to have enjoyed the annual garden parties held at Buckingham Palace*

146 *(Below left) Only Edward VIII demurred. In 1936 he called a halt to the proceedings – some said through boredom, others claimed that he did it to save dresses from being ruined by the rain*

147 *(Below right) George VI talks to Maurice Tate, Patsy Hendren and Frank Woolley at the Oval in 1946 during the centenary celebrations of the cricket ground*

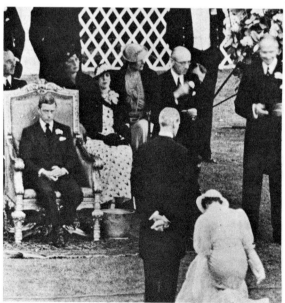

48 *The emergence of radio and television made an enormous difference to the task of meeting the people. In 1933 the Duke of York had been filmed in an instructional documentary on 'safety first'. His daughter became quickly familiar with the new means of communication*

149 (Left) The televising of the Coronation in June 1953 was but one such event. In October she met Sir John Hunt, the conqueror of Everest, before the television cameras at the première of the Everest film

150 At times of disaster, as at times of triumph, the House of Windsor has its role to play. In 1953 Queen Elizabeth, together with Prince Philip and the Duke of Gloucester, visited flood-devastated King's Lynn in Norfolk

Chapter Four

War

The House of Windsor has survived two World Wars in triumph. While Romanovs, Hapsburgs, Hohenzollerns, Ottoman Emperors and Balkan monarchs have fallen like nine-pins, the British royal house has emerged from both global holocausts more secure than ever in the affections of its subjects. The modern British monarchy's lack of real political power no doubt chiefly explains its capacity for adaptation and organic growth, and thus its ability to catch and to reflect the national mood. But there is perhaps more to it than that.

In wartime a constitutional monarchy has several crucial functions to perform. It must help in the mobilization of patriotic and nationalist sentiment; it must intensify, adapt and diversify the performance of its public duties; it must continue, when necessary, to encourage, warn and advise the ministers of the crown. Also, since sovereigns and their families are, after all, men and women, they may wish to play as active a part as possible in the belligerencies. In two World Wars the House of Windsor has acquitted itself most honourably.

King George V had personal reasons for deploring the outbreak of war in 1914, since his second son Prince Albert (the future George VI) was on active service with the Royal Navy. The King's diary for 4 August 1914 records: 'I held a Council at 10.45 to declare war with Germany. It is a terrible catastrophe, but it is not our fault. . . . Please God it may soon be over & that he will protect dear Bertie's life.'

Prince Albert did indeed survive the war, and was present at the long-awaited battle between the Royal Navy and the German High Seas fleet on 31 May 1916. Though the Battle of Jutland was no twentieth-century Trafalgar, the fact that the King's second son served as a sub-lieutenant on board H.M.S. *Collingwood*, which was heavily attacked during the brief action, was the clearest proof of the wholehearted involvement of the House of Windsor in the war. After the Battle of Jutland Prince Albert gave his parents a first-hand account of his experiences: 'I was sitting at the top of A turret and had a very good view of the proceedings. I was up there during a lull, when a German ship started firing at us, and one salvo "straddled" us. . . . I was distinctly startled and jumped down the hole in the top turret like a shot rabbit!! . . . It was certainly a great experience to have been through and it shows we are at war and that the Germans can fight if they want.'

The Prince of Wales served as aide-de-camp to the personal staff of the Commander-in-Chief in France, and subsequently as a staff officer in the Mediterranean and Italy. But he was not allowed to play a fuller part in the fighting. Lord Kitchener of Khartoum, Secretary of State for War from 1914 to 1916, put the position brusquely when he pointed out that although it was of no great consequence if the heir to the throne was killed or wounded, his capture would be a diplomatic disaster for the Allies.

Prince Edward was thus obliged to undertake comparatively 'safe' duties and to chafe at the restrictions imposed by his royal birth. As it was, he tried to get as near the front line as possible, and many of the senior officers responsible for his security would have echoed General Sir Frederick Maude's sentiments on hearing the Prince was being transferred to another command: 'Thank Heavens he's going', Maude had said. 'This job will turn my hair grey. . . . He insists on tramping in the front lines.' Despite his lack of freedom of movement, the Prince of Wales still managed to make contact with a good many of the front-line troops, with whom he became a popular and well-known figure.

George V visited the armies in France five times during the war. He early on formed a low opinion of the British Commander-in-Chief, Sir John French, and became convinced that he should be sacked. In December 1915 the King urged the Prime Minister, Asquith, to appoint Sir Douglas Haig in French's place, and was delighted when this promotion took place shortly afterwards.

The King's visits to the battle areas were not without their risks, and in October 1915 he was badly injured when his chestnut mare slipped and pinned him beneath her; his pelvis was fractured in two places and there was serious and widespread bruising. He suffered agonies for several days and could not even hobble with the aid of sticks until four weeks later.

These injuries, together with the incessant strain placed upon him by the demands of the war, left him a markedly older and frailer man when peace came. During the war he paid seven visits to British naval bases, held 450 inspections, conferred 50,000 decorations with his own hands and visited 300 hospitals. In addition he frequently toured the vitally important industrial regions, the army training grounds and the bombed areas, as well as meeting a steady flow of foreign dignitaries, diplomats and brass-hats.

In 1915, at the behest of Lloyd George, then Minister for Munitions, he also made a private sacrifice. Lloyd George was convinced that drunkenness among the munitions workers was damaging output; he therefore urged the King to set a good example by becoming a teetotaller for the duration of the war; this King George did, though grumbling in his diary: 'I hate doing it, but hope it will do good.'

The women of the royal family also did their bit during the Great War. It was unthinkable that Queen Mary should accompany her husband on all his visits to France and Flanders, but there was plenty of 'woman's work' at home. The Queen and her daughter, Princess Mary, spent countless hours arranging for the despatch of presents to the troops, visiting the war wounded, serving in soup kitchens and inspecting hospitals. The visits to the terribly maimed survivors of the battlefields were undoubtedly ordeals which had to be borne with cheery stoicism, but the Queen's real feelings were revealed in a letter to her son Prince Henry (who was under military age) in November 1916: 'We have rebegun visiting hospitals!!! Oh! dear, oh! dear.'

At the outbreak of the Second World War in September 1939, King George VI had no sons burning to see some action. He had, however, two daughters, and times had changed from 1914–18; Princess Margaret was only nine years old in 1939, but Princess Elizabeth was thirteen, and before the end of the war she had been allowed to join the A.T.S. (the Auxiliary Territorial Service). She entered the A.T.S. records as 'No. 230873 Second

152 On the eve of the Great War: a photograph dated 1913 from the Duke of Windsor's own album. It was Kitchener who prevented the young Prince of Wales from rushing to the front the following year

Papa. Self. Ld. Kitchener. Bertie. Mar

153 *The Prince of Wales eventually made it to France,*
where his recklessness terrified all. In 1917, however, he
was safely behind the lines with his mother at Montigny

Subaltern Elizabeth Alexandra Mary Windsor. Age 18. Eyes, blue. Hair brown. Height 5 ft. 3 in.' Second Subaltern Elizabeth Windsor proceeded to learn how to drive, plunged into axle grease, changed lorry wheels and generally entered into her new duties with zest. Once a senior A.T.S. officer asked the Queen if Princess Elizabeth talked much about her training at home. 'Well,' said her mother, 'last night we had sparking plugs during the whole of dinner!'

The King's brothers made their own contributions to the war effort. The Duke of Windsor, who before the war had been suspected of pro-German leanings and who had visited Hitler at Berchtesgarden in October 1937, immediately offered his services to his homeland. After much official humming and hahing, and a brief and unhappy sojourn in Madrid in 1940, the Duke, accompanied by the Duchess, eventually left to take up the Governorship of the Bahamas. Unpleasant rumours of the Duke's desire for a peaceful settlement with Germany, and of the Duchess's friendship with the Nazi leader Ribbentrop, were not, however, immediately dispelled by his evident dedication to the cause of the British Empire.

Of the King's other brothers, Prince Henry, Duke of Gloucester, had been gazetted Major-General in January 1937; as a professional soldier, he was appointed Chief Liaison Officer to the British Expeditionary Force in France in 1939. In 1942 Sir John Wardlaw-Milne, an influential Conservative MP, proposed that the Duke be made Commander-in-Chief of the British Army – thus harking back to the controversial tenure of that defunct office by Queen Victoria's cousin, the second Duke of Cambridge, from 1856 to 1895; Wardlaw-Milne's proposal was greeted with some unkindly derision in the House of Commons, and no more was heard of it.

The Duke of Kent, the King's youngest brother, was Governor-General designate of Australia when war broke out. He at once asked for duties nearer home, and was appointed Air Commodore in the Royal Air Force. In August 1942, while on a tour of R.A.F. establishments, his Sunderland Flying Boat crashed in the Scottish Highlands and he was killed. Like so many of his subjects, the King thus lost a brother killed while on active service.

The tragic death of the Duke of Kent increased Queen Elizabeth's disquiet at the flights the King was obliged to make during the war. But it was not only those on active service who faced danger during the conflict. The Blitz, and later the V.1 and V.2 raids, caused heavy civilian casualties. During the Blitz the King and Queen made many unheralded visits to damaged areas, where on one occasion a man called out 'Thank God for a good King', and King George replied 'Thank God for a good people'.

Nothing could have more clearly symbolized the House of Windsor's identification with their peoples' war than the sharing of common dangers. Though Princess Elizabeth and Princess Margaret naturally spent a good deal of time in the comparative safety of Windsor, the King and the Queen stayed resolutely in the capital. With a determination equivalent to that of the Prime Minister Winston Churchill (though less eloquent) the King proposed to fight to the bitter end, a revolver in his hand, in Buckingham Palace. On 9 September 1940 a bomb fell on the north side of the palace, and three days later six bombs struck the chapel, the garden, the forecourt and the quadrangle. No lives were lost, but, as the King wrote: 'It was a ghastly experience & I don't want it to be repeated.'

While the King and his immediate family were facing hazards in Britain, two Mountbatten cousins were on active service. Of these, the senior, Lord Louis Mountbatten, ended the war as the Supreme Allied Commander in South-East Asia. His nephew, Philip, whose bearded photograph adorned Princess Elizabeth's room, eventually rose to the post of First Lieutenant on the destroyer H.M.S. *Whelp*.

Like his father before him, King George VI bore a colossal burden during the war. His visits were many: to the B.E.F., to the Fleet, to devastated Coventry and other bombed areas, to North Africa, to Malta, to Normandy shortly after D-Day, to Italy and the Low Countries. He also enjoyed a close working relationship with Winston Churchill, with whom he lunched once a week, and to whom he sent frequent letters of thoughtful advice over the prosecution of the war. While their relationship was in general strikingly harmonious, the King had a hard tussle to prevent his Prime Minister from accompanying the troops on the D-Day invasion; King George had also expressed a similar wish, but his Private Secretary, Sir Alan Lascelles, strongly objected to such an enterprise. The King subsequently badgered Churchill into abandoning his original plan, and finally received the not ungracious reply that 'I must defer to Your Majesty's wishes & indeed commands. It is a great comfort to me to know that they arise from Your Majesty's desire to keep me in your service. ... Your Majesty's humble & devoted Servant and Subject (signed) Winston S. Churchill'.

At last, in August 1945, the Second World War came to an end, and, in common with their subjects, the House of Windsor turned to deal with the perplexing problems of the post-war environment. The royal family had indeed played the fullest possible part in the struggle. After the Great War, David Lloyd George had said of King George V's role in that conflict: 'There can be no question that one outstanding reason for the high level of loyalty and patriotic effort which the people of this country maintained was the attitude and conduct of King George.' The same could have been said of King George VI in 1945.

154 Prince Albert (Duke of York) joined the Royal Navy and as a sub-lieutenant fought on H.M.S. Collingwood at the Battle of Jutland

155 His health, however, suffered and he was called home. He serves tea to wounded men at Buckingham Palace

156 (Below) The House of Windsor's involvement in the First World War was mainly borne by the King and Queen. In 1915 George V visited many of the battle areas in France before being badly injured when his chestnut mare slipped and pinned him beneath her

157 *By 1917 he was active enough to visit a submarine*   158 *(Right) He also took an interest in the air war, visiting a London aerodrome in the same year*

159 *Hospital visits were on the agenda of every member of the royal family. In 1918 Queen Mary presented pipes and tobacco to wounded soldiers at Richmond*

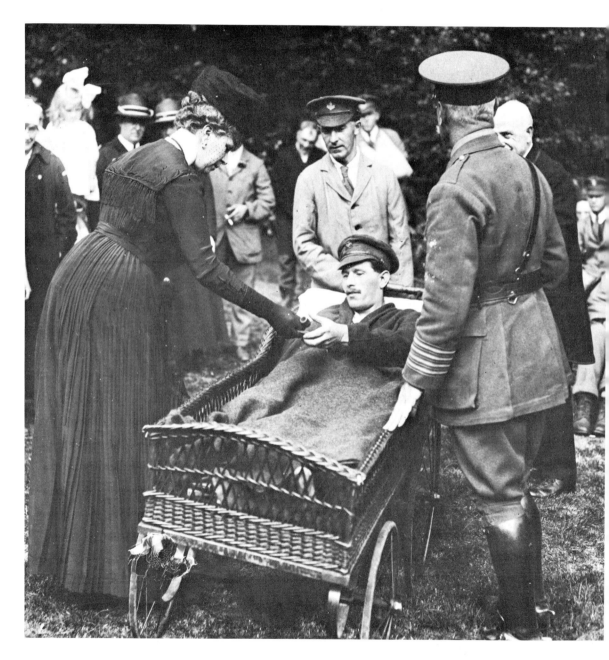

160 *On a secret visit to France in July the previous year
he talked to gunners before they rejoined the firing line*

161 (Left) The value of home front produce, dead or
alive, had been forcefully brought home as a result of the
submarine war

162 In 1918 George V is shown with (left to right)
Joffre, Poincaré, Foch and Haig

*163 The war over, the King and the Duke of York visit
British soldiers' graves at Ypres*

164 *In 1922 the King and Queen visited the Nurse Cavell memorial*

165 *After strained years of peace, there came again rumours of war. In 1935 the old King carried out his last military duties when he visited the RAF base at Mildenhall in Suffolk*

166 *(Below left) George VI now took on the mantle of his father. He visited in 1938 the RAF base at Northolt*

167 *(Below right) Together with Queen Elizabeth he talked to army officers at Aldershot*

168 When war came, opportunities for movement abroad became necessarily restricted. The slow start, however, enabled the King to visit the French Army zone with General Gamelin, Commander in Chief of the Allied Armies, in December 1939

169 The King also reviewed the British Expeditionary Force

170 In August 1940 the King welcomed to England General Sikorsky, Commander in Chief of the Polish forces in exile

171 Much later, in October 1944 when the tide of war had irreversibly turned, he toured the battlefronts of France with General Eisenhower

*172 In June 1943 the King met Generals Giraud and
de Gaulle during his tour of North Africa. General
Alexander is on the left*

173 In the same month the King had ventured into the Mediterranean. The royal car passed through the bomb-scarred but cheerfully crowded streets of Valetta, capital of the George Cross island, Malta

174–5 *If Hitler had the resources of Europe to draw upon,*
Britain could look to the Empire. The King reviews
Canadian troops based in southern England and rides in a
carrier during the same visit, early 1940

176 North Africa, June 1943

178 Queen Mary talks to Indian troops at Overseas House in London

177 (Below) With General Montgomery, the King drives past fighter aircraft of the Desert Air Force and acknowledges the cheers of the ground crews

179 Montgomery, newly appointed Field Marshal, introduces his dog 'Hitler' to the King, October 1944

180 A visit to a night fighter station – recorded with the aid of an infra-red plate, May 1941

181 With Air Chief Marshal Sir Hugh Dowding at Fighter Command headquarters, September 1939

182 With Flight-Lieutenant John Carrington DFC, DSO, a crack night fighter pilot, just before take-off

183 *The King was rather less involved with the Navy in the Second World War than he had been in the First. He is shown relaxing at an ENSA show in March 1943*

184 *November 1944: the King inspects the plotting room in Portsmouth from which the shipping operations for D-Day were controlled*

185 One of the most important roles of the House of Windsor during the Second World War was to encourage the Home Front. The King broadcast regularly to Britain and the Empire

186 The King is stopped by Land Defence Volunteers (soon to become the Home Guard) at Woodford

187 *'Farmer George' was an image carefully fostered to encourage home production*

189 *The two Princesses 'dug for Victory' on their own allotment*

188 *Examining a crop of barley at Windsor*

190 *Stirrup-pump practice for the royal family – a precautionary measure in the event of fire*

191 *In September 1940 Buckingham Palace was hit by bombs and the House of Windsor became more closely than ever identified with the people*

192 *Meeting demolition workers during a tour of London's bombed areas*

193 *Despite the stress of war, cheerfulness kept breaking out*

194 *Princess Elizabeth gave her first broadcast on 13 October 1940 during 'Children's Hour'. Princess Margaret listens*

195 *(Right) March 1945: Princess Elizabeth in her ATS uniform – a powerful aid to recruiting*

196 (Left) As an ATS Officer, Princess Elizabeth talked knowledgeably of sparking plugs

197 The Duke of Windsor in January 1940, waiting in London for the call to duty

198 The call, when it came, was to the Bahamas; the Duke was appointed Governor-General and the Duchess became President of the Bahamas branch of the British Red Cross

199–200 Lord Louis Mountbatten, Supreme Allied Commander in South East Asia, talks to sailors in Ceylon and soldiers in Burma, early 1945

201 The Duchess of Kent at a Chelsea first-aid post in 1940

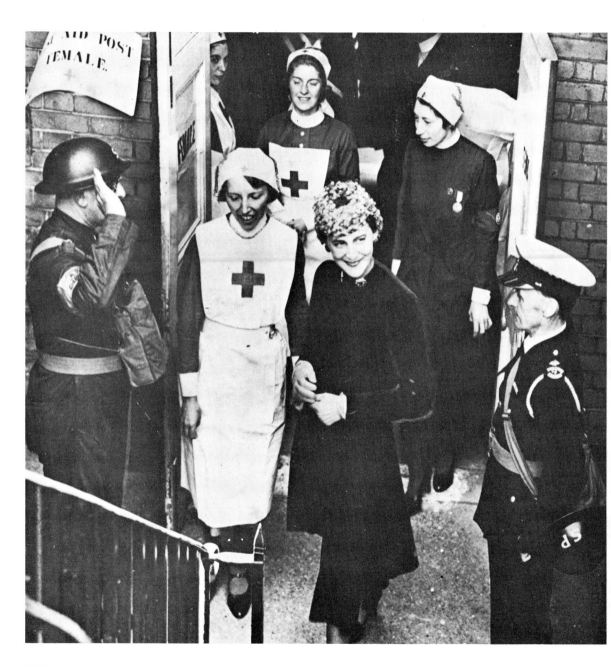

202 The Duke of Kent addresses American aircraft
workers in Baltimore, September 1941. He was to die
in a tragic air crash the following year

203 The Duchess of Kent visits the United Nations
Forces Club in St James's Square, November 1943

204 *The end of the war: the royal procession moves down Ludgate Circus after the national thanksgiving service in St Paul's Cathedral*

205 *On the balcony of Buckingham Palace, on VE Day 1945, the hero of the hour, Winston Churchill, was given the central position*

206 *By the time of the VJ celebrations in August, Churchill was out of office and a new Labour government under Attlee installed*

208–9 *Old VC's never die and in 1956 Queen Elizabeth
inspected veterans from all parts of Britain and the
Commonwealth, at a special Victoria Cross parade in
Hyde Park*

Chapter Five

Ambassadors

Monarchs enjoy a considerable, and perhaps inflated, reputation as ambassadors in their country's interests. Edward VII is popularly supposed to have laid the foundations of the Anglo-French entente by his remarkably successful official visit to Paris in 1903; in fact, the British and French governments had since 1901 been discussing ways of reducing tension between the two countries; King Edward's Parisian triumph merely added some icing to the carefully baked diplomatic cake. Sometimes, of course, monarchs can be rank bad ambassadors, or indeed non-ambassadors: the Prince Regent, for example, never forgave the Tsar Alexander I for his rudeness during the latter's visit to England in 1814; Queen Victoria was hardly a globe-trotter, and Balmoral in the north and Osborne in the south were the two poles of her peregrinations.

Even George V, the founder of the House of Windsor, did not travel extensively after his accession and developed a deep-rooted objection to trips to the continent of Europe. In 1925 he refused point blank to undertake a State Visit to Spain and argued that 'State Visits have ceased to be of any political importance'. In the same year he grudgingly agreed on a Mediterranean cruise in the interests of his health, but made it plain that he would have preferred to stay at home.

This insularity of outlook contrasts oddly with King George's former seafaring life and his earlier missions to Berlin, Madrid, Vienna and Paris. Between 1901 and 1906, moreover, he and Princess Mary visited Gibraltar, Malta, Aden, Ceylon, Singapore, Australia, New Zealand, Mauritius, Natal, the Cape, Canada, Newfoundland and the Indian Empire; in 1911–12, as King-Emperor, he returned to India to hold a Coronation Durbar. As Duke of York, and later as Prince of Wales, he no doubt felt obliged to undertake visits on behalf of his grandmother and father; he was also far more involved with imperial than with foreign affairs, and this explains his determination to return to India in 1911.

Nor should it be forgotten that George V visited the Empire's armies in France five times during the Great War. That he was a great success on these trips is evident from his own account of his visit to the battle areas in France and Belgium after the armistice: 'At each place I got out & walked through the troops who cheered me. It was not stiff, the men often following me through the town.' In 1921 the King made another foray, in the cause of duty, to Belfast; there he opened the new parliament of Ulster, and in so doing made a powerful speech designed to help bind up the wounds of a bitterly divided Ireland. That he risked assassination during his trip to Ulster is an indication of how keenly he felt that the Irish people, both north and south, were *his* people, and consequently worthy of special attention.

But generally in the postwar years King George had one excellent reason for staying put

210 Berlin 1913: the personal diplomacy of George V and Queen Mary counted for little in the events to come

211–12 Berlin 1937: the Duke of Windsor's contacts
were equally ineffectual. Dr Robert Ley, Reich Labour
Minister under Hitler, shows the ex-King round a car
factory

at home: he could dispatch his sons to the four corners of the earth as ambassadors on his behalf. The most celebrated, and controversial, ambassador of them all was the Prince of Wales. In 1919 Prince Edward visited Newfoundland, Canada and the United States. A year later he toured Australia and New Zealand, via the West Indies, Honolulu and Fiji, and at the end of 1921 he set out to visit India.

This latter tour demonstrated the serious limitations of such ventures. While it had been a simple matter to enchant Australian, Canadian or even American spectators, Indian nationalism was in the process of being mobilized by Gandhi's non-violent non-cooperation movement. The foundations of the Raj were, indeed, already badly damaged and could certainly not be repaired by the transitory presence of a slim, short, active young man with a charming, shy smile, who nervously fingered his tie and smoked cigarettes rather too frequently. Gandhi's appeal for a boycott of the tour was highly successful in many places. In Bombay thousands of placards condemned the visit; in Calcutta there were as many jeers as cheers; in Madras there was arson and window-smashing and pictures of the Prince were trampled on.

Yet despite the cat-calls, the closed shops and the often sullen crowds, the Prince of Wales managed to convey his sincerity and charm to those who cared to take notice. Earlier in Australia the *Sydney Sun* had remarked that 'Before the Prince landed the popular idea of princes was of something haughty and remote, but this smiling, appealing youthful man smiled away the differences which Australians believed lay between royalty and the common people'.

In 1924 Prince Edward went to the United States for the second time, and a year later sailed for South Africa, stopping at the Gold Coast and Nigeria en route. Later he visited South America. He was by no means an entirely willing royal tourist, and before his 1921 trip to India, for example, had indicated that the prospect did not please him, only to be put in his place by his father who said: 'I don't care whether the PM wants you to go or not. *I* wish you to go, and you are going.'

The Prince of Wales, like other members of the Windsor family before and after him, suffered bouts of exhaustion and depression while on tour. He also paid a heavy price in terms of his father's regard for him. King George was at best a loving, though demanding, parent; but he was also a stickler for etiquette and found it difficult to approve of many of the phenomena of the 'flapper era'. He accordingly followed his son's deportment overseas with an eagle eye, and a great deal of what he saw displeased him. He tended to overlook the praise lavished on his son by local dignitaries and to dwell instead on allegations of royal flippancy and occasional lapses of decorum. For King George, the unwelcome vulgarity of modern times was epitomized in the headlines with which American newspapers had greeted his eldest son: 'Here he is girls – the most eligible bachelor yet uncaught.' 'Oh! Who'll ask HRH what he wears asleep?' 'Prince of Wales has 'em guessing in the wee hours.'

George V, however, considered his second son, Prince Albert, to be the epitome of rectitude and commonsense, 'very different to dear David' (the Prince of Wales). Prince Albert also bore his share of ambassadorial trips. While Duke of York he visited Brussels, Yugoslavia (twice), Ulster, East Africa, the Sudan, Australia, New Zealand, Denmark, Norway and Italy; he also undertook a world tour in 1927 which, apart from Australia and New

Zealand, took him to Las Palmas, the West Indies, Panama, Fiji, Mauritius, Port Said, Malta and Gibraltar. King George, however, was no more lavish in his praise for Prince Albert's efforts than he had been for those of the Prince of Wales.

Markedly as the Duke of York's speech impediment had begun to improve after 1926 under the tutelage of the successful specialist, Lionel Logue, royal tours were bound to provide him with an exceptionally heavy burden. In his quiet and dignified way, and possessing the instinct for appropriate informality, the Duke made an extremely favourable impression, especially on his world tour in 1927. He was notably sustained by the responsive and radiant personality of his wife. Indeed in Auckland the royal couple apparently made a dramatic conversion when an erstwhile Communist confessed: 'Yesterday I was in the crowd with the wife, and one of the children waved his hand, and I'm blessed if the Duchess didn't wave back and smile right into my face, not two yards away. I'll never say a word against them again. I've done with it for good and all.'

Posterity does not record the duration of this remarkable volte-face, neither do psephologists show a general swing from the political left, or indeed any significant shift in opinion, in the wake of royal tours. King George VI's visit to Canada and the United States in May and June 1939 did not bring America into the war at Britain's heels three months later; and when in 1947, at General Smuts's behest, the royal family toured South Africa, the election results in the following year were a triumph for the Afrikaner-dominated, anti-British, Nationalist Party.

The 1947 tour of South Africa and the Rhodesias imposed something more than the usual strains upon the royal family. The King was well aware that Britain was in the grip of a serious winter fuel crisis, and was acutely sensitive to criticisms that he should be at his people's side at home; yet he was also King of South Africa, and Briton, Afrikaner, Zulu, Basuto, Xhosa and the rest were equally his subjects. For Princess Elizabeth the tour must have seemed like a further postponement of her marriage to Philip Mountbatten; her father was well aware of her feelings, and in a letter written to his daughter shortly after her wedding referred to her 'long wait', and added: 'I was so anxious for you to come to South Africa as you knew. Our family, us four, the "Royal Family" must remain together with additions of course at suitable moments!!'

Princess Elizabeth in fact made a significant and historic broadcast while in South Africa. On 21 April 1947 she came of age, and delivered, in a clear and patently sincere voice, the following message to the people of the Commonwealth and Empire: 'I declare before you all that my whole life, whether it be long or short, shall be devoted to your service and the service of our great Imperial Commonwealth to which we all belong.'

With her father's health failing, Princess Elizabeth and her new husband were soon to carry out royal tours in their own right. On 7 October 1951 they left for a tour of Canada and a visit to the United States. The seriousness of the King's condition (his left lung had been removed in an operation on 23 September 1951) obliged Princess Elizabeth to take with her a sealed envelope, containing the draft Accession Declaration and a Message to both Houses of Parliament, to be opened only if her father died. But he did not die, and her first independent mission overseas was an unqualified success; the royal couple spent thirty-five days in North America, travelled nearly 10,000 miles in Canada alone, and visited every province of the Dominion.

213 *Years before, in 1922, Edward had visited Japan (with his staff)*

214 *The scars of war were healing when Prince Akihito of Japan joined the Queen in the royal box at Epsom in 1953*

215 *Princess Elizabeth moves through the halls of the Vatican to meet the Pope, April 1951*

216 *(Right) Italian contacts were limited, but in 1924 the Queen of Italy and the Queen of England together walked under an umbrella at the Wembley Exhibition*

Five months later, on 31 January 1952, they set off for a Commonwealth tour of East Africa, Australia and New Zealand. King George VI, hatless and windswept, had waved them goodbye at London airport. In the early morning of 6 February he died peacefully in his sleep.

Queen Elizabeth II now succeeded not only to the throne but to the full ardours of State Visits and Royal Tours. Soon after her accession she became the most travelled monarch in British history. Quite apart from State Visits to foreign capitals, she has been to Canada six times, Australia, New Zealand and Fiji three times, Jamaica, Tonga and Malta twice, and almost every part of the Commonwealth at least once. It is an irony of history that as Empire has faded into Commonwealth, the British royal family have visited with extraordinary consistency the territories over which the Union Jack once flew.

Some of these tours have been staggering in their scope. The six-month Commonwealth Tour of 1953, for example, involved the Queen and the Duke of Edinburgh in 19,307 miles of travel by sea, 17,267 by air, 3,600 by car and 1,500 by train. In 1961 there was a three-week tour of what was once the brightest jewel in the Imperial Crown – India, where the Queen received a reception far more complimentary than that previously dealt out to King-Emperors and their heirs. In the same year she insisted, against official advice, on visiting Ghana, the first black state of British Africa to gain independence.

It is as difficult to gauge the real value of Queen Elizabeth's tours as of those undertaken by her predecessors. The Duke of Edinburgh, indeed, made a characteristically frank attempt to reassess the worth of royal tours in October 1969, telling the Canadians: 'We can think of other ways of enjoying ourselves. Judging by some of the programmes we are required to do here and considering how little we get out of it, you can assume it is done in the interests of the Canadian people and not in our own interests.' He went on: 'If at any time . . . people feel that it [the monarchy] has no future part to play, then for goodness sake let's end the thing on amicable terms without having a row about it.' Certainly, whatever the future holds for royal tours, a good deal of the old formality and stiffness has gone, due in part to the pressures of an increasingly egalitarian age, and in part, perhaps, to the relaxed bearing of the Duke of Edinburgh, who has also often acted as a realistic super-salesman for British exports. Moreover, as the world's number of crowned heads continues to decrease, the sight of a monarch who can trace her descent back to William the Conqueror and King Harold, and is also sixth cousin twice removed from George Washington, is rare enough to justify the occasional royal ambassadorial progress.

217 Of other European countries the relationship with France was perhaps more fruitful. In 1903 King Edward VII had visited Paris on his way to the holiday resort of Biarritz, and his trip was popularly thought to have set the seal on the Entente Cordiale

218 In 1914 George V drove through the streets of Paris with President Poincaré shortly before the war clouds burst

219 *In 1938, again under the shadow of war, George VI and his Queen attend a garden party in the Bois de Boulogne in the company of President Lebrun*

20 Shortly after the war, Princess Elizabeth and Prince Philip were in Paris to open an exhibition called 'Eight Centuries of British Life in France'. The speaker – to whom scant attention is being paid – is Pierre de Gaulle, the General's brother and president of the Paris municipal council

221 *The most celebrated ambassador of them all, Edward, Prince of Wales, visited King Faud in Cairo in 1922*

222 *In 1952 King Faisal of Iraq was entertained at Balmoral*

223 *Marshal Tito of Yugoslavia visited Buckingham Palace in 1952 – thawing out*

224 *The Duke of Gloucester on behalf of the Queen visited President Makarios and Vice-President Kuchuk of Cyprus in 1960*

225 In 1953 the Queen was photographed with her Dominion Prime Ministers and the Chief Minister of Jamaica, Alexander Bustamenta (sixth from left)

226 General Francisco Lopez, the Portuguese President, entertained the Queen and Prince Philip on their visit to Portugal in 1957

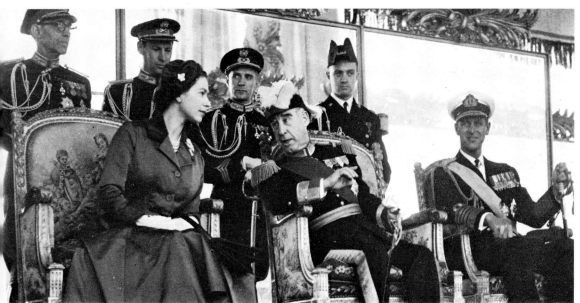

227 (Left) In 1954 the Queen and Prince Philip visited the ruins of the ancient city of Pellonnaruwa in Ceylon

228 A State Banquet with local plenipotentiaries in Kuala Lumpur, Malaya, in 1956 – part of the Duke of Edinburgh's four-month world tour

229 Bearded again, Prince Philip visited Gambia in 1957

230 *The major target of the House of Windsor's ambassadorial role has always been the 'older' Dominions: Canada, South Africa, Australia, and New Zealand. In 1919 the Prince of Wales was rapturously acclaimed by crowds as he left Parliament Buildings in Victoria, Canada*

231 *In 1927 an enthusiastic loyalist brought smiles to the faces of the Duke and Duchess of York on their tour of New Zealand*

232 In 1954 Queen Elizabeth visited a disabled service-men's centre in Christchurch, New Zealand

233 In Sydney, Australia, the Queen was escorted by Prime Minister Menzies to the Lord Mayor's Ball

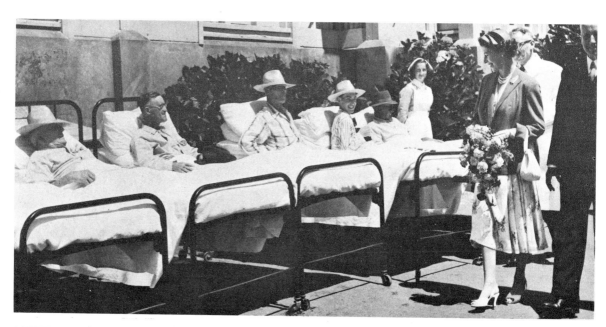

234 *The mascot of the First Battalion of the Royal Australian Infantry attracted the Queen's attention at Brisbane*

235 (Overleaf) *At Brisbane also the Queen and Prince Philip watched aborigines enact a wallaby dance, with mixed reactions*

236 Queen Salote of Tonga refused to put up her umbrella at the Coronation and won the hearts of the London crowds. She had no such inhibitions when the rain poured on the two Queens in Tonga's capital city in December 1953

237 (Below left) In 1947 the royal family visited South Africa. Princess Elizabeth inspects girl guides in Basutoland

238 (Below right) In a Johannesburg gold-mine the royal family descended 7,700 feet

239 *With Field Marshal Smuts, the South African Premier (holding staff), at the top of Table Mountain, Cape Town. Smuts, aged 76, had climbed on foot; the others had gone by cable-car*

240-3 *Incident at Cochrane in Canada: a preliminary*
exchange of telegrams with the local mayor, followed by
the arrival of the royal train, and the presentation by the
artist of his picture (1951)

CANADIAN PACIFIC
TELEGRAPHS
World Wide Communications

W D NEIL GENERAL MANAGER

"The filing time shown in the date line is STANDARD TIME at place of origin. Time of receipt is STANDARD TIME at place of destination."

CR B 35-4 Extra Via Calgary
WOODSTOCK ONT. OCT. 14-820 A

MAYOR G.BROATCH.
COCHRANE. ALTA.

      WOULD BE PLEASED TO HAVE YOU GREET THIER
ROYAL HIGHNESSES ON ARRIVAL AT COCHRANE STOP.SCHEDULE
PERMITS ONLY FEW MINUTES AT THIS POINT SO GREETING
MUST BE BREIF WITHOUT CEREMONEY

                C.STEIN,
                UNDER SECRETARY OF STATE
                CHAIRMAN OF THE SPECIAL COMMITTEE

CANADIAN PACIFIC
TELEGRAPHS
World Wide Communications

W D NEIL GENERAL MANAGER

"The filing time shown in the date line is STANDARD TIME at place of origin. Time of receipt is STANDARD TIME at place of destination."

CR B 16-4 Extra.
ROYAL TRAIN OCT. 17-1015 A

MAYOR GRAEME BROATCH.
COCHRANE. ALTA.

    PERMISSION TO PRESENT T.R.H. WITH PAINTING BY
LOCAL ARTIST UPON ARRIVAL GRANTED.

           C.STEIN,
        UNDER SECRETARY OF STATE,
        CHAIRMAN OF THE SPECIAL COMMITTEE.
1042

244 *(Overleaf left) The Calgary stampede is watched in a snowstorm*

245 *(Overleaf right) In Ottawa the official ball was a barn-dance and Princess Elizabeth's 'square-dance skirt' was to start a fashion*

246 Outside of the Commonwealth the most determined ambassadorial efforts have always been directed at the United States. In May 1939 the King and Queen left for North America – a timely attempt, perhaps, to influence American public opinion

247 (Below left) There the King listened to President Roosevelt

248 (Below right) Later, in 1942, the King and Queen greeted Mrs Roosevelt on arrival in London

249 *Visiting an Indian encampment outside Calgary on the North American tour*

250 *A pause for photographic reflection on the same tour*

251 *In 1951 President Truman greeted Princess Elizabeth at Washington*

252 *And the Queen was welcomed back in 1957*

253 *(Overleaf left) President Eisenhower talked to the Queen in the White House*

254 *(Overleaf right) While Vice-President Nixon and his wife showed the visitors round the Capitol*

Chapter Six
Sports and Pastimes

If the traditional relaxations and pastimes of the House of Windsor were to be expressed in heraldic form, a number of predictable items would appear: horses rampant, of course; crossed twelve-bore shot guns; 'penny blacks' couchant; polo sticks, spinnakers, assorted dogs, some objets d'art, a few theatre tickets, a biography or two.

The royal family's pastimes are essentially those of the aristocracy of which it nowadays forms the most important part. Although in recent years the driving of fast sports cars and the taking of highly professional photographs have entered the family repertoire, there is nothing particularly breathtaking or scandalous about the relaxations of rather longer standing. The House of Windsor has, thankfully, not produced a mad King Ludwig of Bavaria or a Catherine the Great. Even its blood sports have been reasonably clean-cut and home-grown.

George V, direct, monogamous, meticulous and somewhat humdrum, lived an orderly life that contrasted sharply with the raffish and hedonistic pursuits of his father Edward VII. King George lived his life according to the book – it was, on the whole, a good book, but not all his family wished to stick so closely to the rules and regulations of the text. He ate his plain meals at the same time every day; preferred to go to bed at ten minutes past eleven o'clock every night; he was also suspicious of and steadfastly resistant to change, especially in his private world, and frequently harkened back to the naturally unrepeatable days of his late-Victorian youth.

His hobbies and pastimes were few, but carried to the point of excellence. He was a first-class shot and revelled in the dextrous slaughter of a wide variety of animals and birds. When in 1911 he and Queen Mary travelled to India for the Coronation Durbar, he insisted that the already heavy itinerary should include a week's tiger-shooting, thus provoking the Secretary of State for India, Lord Crewe, to observe wryly: 'It is a misfortune for a public personage to have any taste so strongly developed as the craze for shooting is in our beloved Ruler.'

King George was also one of the world's leading philatelists, though it must be admitted that, as a prince and later King-Emperor, he was supremely well placed to make a huge stamp collection. He was in addition an accomplished yachtsman and was devoted to Cowes week. In 1893 he acquired the *Britannia* and sailed her with love and enthusiasm until the end of his life; by 1934 she had competed in 569 races, had won 231 First Prizes and 124 other prizes; as befitted the craft of a sailor King, she was towed out to a point south of the Isle of Wight, five months after her master's death, and given a naval burial!

The King's extraordinarily retentive memory and sharp nautical eye were reflected in his interest in anniversaries and statistics, and also in his almost obsessional concern over correctness of dress. In the latter respect he was peculiarly exacting, a trait he had inherited from his father and was to pass on to his son George VI. Generally, he disapproved of new fashions in clothes, and even of new dance steps; once in the 1920s he came across Queen Mary diffidently practising the latest dance routine and exploded in wrath.

Queen Mary, in fact, though of a conservative and inhibited disposition, had very different tastes from her husband. Early in her marriage she had announced her intention of 'improving her mind', and she continued to read seriously (often in history) throughout her life. She undoubtedly felt some annoyance, though admirably controlled, at the philistine tendencies of the 'Wales cousins' – the three sisters of George V. When, before the royal trip to India in 1911, the King was concerned with arranging a tiger shoot, Queen Mary read instructive books to prepare for her visits to Agra and the Taj Mahal. In 1925 a cruise to the Mediterranean to restore the King's health was, in one respect, a disaster, for though the Queen wished to see Italian and Sicilian antiquities, her husband and his sister Princess Victoria did not, and when persuaded to go kept up a barrage of disrespectful chaff.

Two other hobbies of Queen Mary's are worth mentioning. One was her taste for collecting and rearranging furniture and works of art; Windsor Castle eventually housed the bulk of her acquisitions. The Queen's collection, though valuable, did not necessarily reflect an incisive aesthetic sense or a sure grasp of long-term artistic trends; still, it gave her inordinate satisfaction. So, too, did her doll's house. Designed by Sir Edwin Lutyens, one of the architects of the somewhat larger project of New Delhi, the doll's house was presented to Queen Mary by Princess Marie-Louise, a granddaughter of Queen Victoria and known to the family as 'Cousin Louie'. Built on four floors and able to accommodate a family six inches tall, the doll's house was a great success at the 1924 Wembley Exhibition and was later installed in a special room at Windsor Castle.

Such delightful fripperies aside, Queen Mary was apparently content to follow a staid and conventional routine for most of her married life. Though she loved the theatre and dancing, the King, especially in his later years, preferred to stay at home, and she was obliged to stay with him. Her eldest son, however, was no stay-at-home. In the interwar years the Prince of Wales' social life centred on fast cars, night clubs, dancing into the early hours, and the company of young people considered by his father to be both frivolous and fast. His brother George, Duke of Kent, had tastes compatible with his own; his brothers Albert, Duke of York, and Henry, Duke of Gloucester, did not.

The Prince of Wales had other, more serious, pastimes. He was a courageous, though not particularly successful, steeplechase rider; he learnt to fly; he played golf (and the bagpipes); he also loved gardening at Fort Belvedere, a royal house six miles from Windsor. Weekend parties were equally part of his tenure of Fort Belvedere, something his father had suspected when he asked if he could have the house. 'What could you possibly want that old place for?' the King had said. 'Those damn weekends, I suppose.'

George VI's private relaxations were much more akin to his father's. He, too, was an excellent marksman and spent his last day of life at his beloved Sandringham shooting hares. His interest in estate management would have made him a first-rate and progressive squire. He was also devoted to gardening and spent many hours digging, tending bonfires and planting. Indeed his son-in-law, the Duke of Edinburgh, recollects that he first met King George when the latter was hacking, and swearing, at a rhododendron bush.

256 Reloading during a tiger shoot in Nepal

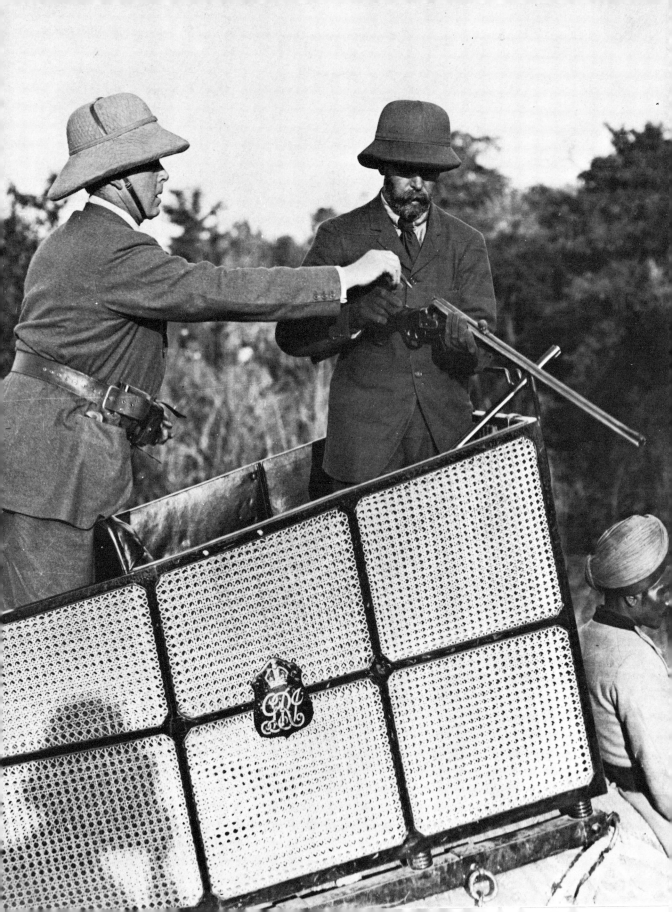

George VI, like his male ancestors from 1782 onwards, was a dedicated Freemason. He was also very interested in industrial welfare; he frequently met captains of industry and trade union leaders, and visited countless factories though later recalling: 'It seems that I place an evil spell on machines. . . . Once to my surprise and dismay, I was dropped in a lift. Another time a fool-proof stamping machine threw out forty unstamped letters for my benefit. The threads of looms seem to break whenever I approach.' As Duke of York he established in 1921 an annual holiday camp in which an equal number of boys from industry and the public schools lived and worked together for a week.

Matters of dress were as important to King George VI as to his father. He was an expert on decorations, and liable to point out the smallest sartorial irregularity. Once he asked his godson King Peter of Yugoslavia whether a slender gold watch chain was part of the uniform of the Royal Yugoslav Air Force. On receiving a negative reply, he said: 'Take it off. It looks damned silly and damned sloppy.'

The King had a racy sense of humour, though perhaps less ribald than his father's, and was a devotee of Tommy Handley's I.T.M.A. He was apt to collapse in irrepressible laughter at family jokes. It seems that he much appreciated his younger daughter's quick wit and gift of mimicry as much as her talent for piano playing.

His eldest daughter, the future Queen Elizabeth, was of a less mercurial, more serious turn of mind. Her main private relaxation was, and is, to be in the open air, preferably somewhere near a horse. She is an expert horsewoman (an interest conspicuously shared by Princess Anne) and a shrewd judge of horse flesh. She has had a number of successes with her race horses. Otherwise her pastimes are not particularly extraordinary: family picnics, dogs, Scottish country dancing, driving, farming techniques, walking, and a modest amount of television-watching, theatre- and cinema-going, and reading.

The Duke of Edinburgh is a little more unorthodox, obstinately continuing to play polo, the great sport of the vanished Indian Raj, and espousing conservation before it became fashionable – though his earlier prowess with the gun moved the League Against Cruel Sports to describe him as 'trigger-happy' and once, after the slaughter of 650 birds in a day's shooting with the Italian tycoon Vittorio Necchi, a newspaper denounced his activities as 'butchery'. He also has a genuine interest in industrial efficiency and in scientific and technological developments. He enjoys writing, and delivering, his own speeches, and has made some adept appearances on television. Moreover, he has fostered his reputation as a speaker of home truths and the deliverer of national pep-talks, all of which he does with ability and panache, as when he told a gathering of manufacturers that 'It is no good shutting your eyes, saying "Britain is best" three times a day and expecting it to be so'.

There are other members of the present House of Windsor with similarly diverse tastes and interests. Lord Snowdon has introduced talents of an artistic, not to say bohemian, character; Lord Harewood, the Queen's cousin, has an intense and long-standing preoccupation with the world of good music; Princess Anne wears hats that would have outraged her maternal great-grandfather; Prince Charles has his pilot's wings and enjoys archaeological digs and playing the cello. Of course the wearing of fashionable hats, the appreciation of Mozart and a love of horses are not unique or mystical attributes, and in a constitutional monarchy which lurches sporadically towards egalitarianism this is entirely appropriate.

257 George V examines the bag. At the time he was reputed to be one of the four best shots in the country

195

258 (Left) In 1961 the last royal tiger fell to Prince Philip. The noise of the shot was heard around the world

260 He put it into practice in Tanganyika where he shot a fine kudo

259 The Prince of Wales learnt his shooting in Scotland

261 (Below) But for the Prince horses were a more sustaining interest. In 1921 George V and a delighted Queen Mary congratulated him on winning his first race under National Hunt rules

262 *Meanwhile the Duke of York was hunting with the Belvoir at Croxton Park*

263 *He crosses the polo field with his future wife, Lady Elizabeth Bowes-Lyon*

264 *He takes part in a polo match*

265 *He goes (with his wife) to Ascot*

266–7 *Polo was also the forte of Lord Mountbatten, who won the Duke of York Cup in 1931, and of his cousin Prince Philip*

268–9 *The excitement of a horse race grips the spectators – one focuses on the finish, the other on the loose horses*

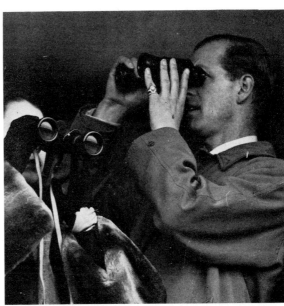

270 The horse has been a constant and reassuring factor in the Queen's life. At the age of four she had riding lessons in Windsor Great Park

271 By the age of thirteen she was a more than competent horsewoman

272 (Below) Royal Ascot 1952

273 *Princess Anne is an outstanding rider by any standards*

274 *Prince Charles, an excellent polo player, unmounts to take up batting!*

275 *Prince Edward sorts out polo sticks for his father and brother at Windsor in 1971*

276 *The House of Windsor were early players of golf but the interest has not been sustained. In 1911 the Duke of York played at Torquay*

277 *He played a more gentle game on his honeymoon*

278 *The Prince of Wales opened the Richmond golf course in 1923 – with a savagely pulled drive that amazed the spectators*

279 *Later he took the game a little more seriously*

280–2 Prince Philip has always been keen on cricket. When he became engaged in 1947 he took a party to Lord's to watch Eton play Harrow. (Below) Practising at Corsham Naval Station

283 (Right) Flying has always been popular with the men of the House of Windsor although it has brought them their share of personal grief. The Duke of Edinburgh flies his plane over Windsor Castle in 1953

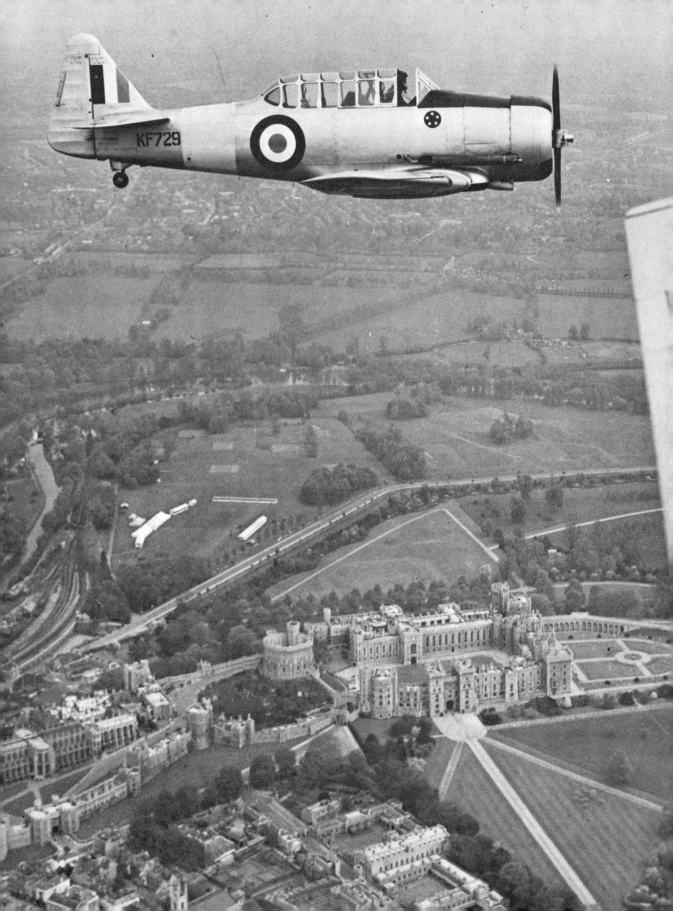

284 Football for the House of Windsor has been mainly a spectator sport. The Prince of Wales kicks off at a match between Tottenham Hotspur and Fulham in 1921

286 (Right) Guiding and scouting have always been popular. The Duke and Duchess of York wore their uniforms at Adelaide in 1927

285 In 1924 the Prince of Wales was at the Paris Olympics

287 *The two Princesses in their Girl Guide uniforms in 1938*

288 *Princess Elizabeth in swimming costume at the Bath Club, London, in 1939*

289 *(Right) George V – at the wheel of Britannia – never missed Regatta Week at Cowes. He remained an inveterate sailor*

290 *The Duke of Edinburgh aboard the yacht* Bluebottle *in 1948*

291 *Prince Charles sails* Coweslip *in 1971*

292 *At various times every member of the House of Windsor has tried his hand at fishing. The Duke of York landed a ground shark in New Zealand in 1927*

293 *In the previous year he had played in the Wimbledon championships*

294 *The Masonic Movement, which the Duke of York joined at Glamis in June 1936, proved of lasting interest to him*

295 *Princess Elizabeth's piano playing was always enjoyed by her parents*

296 *Edward's defiant playing of the bagpipes was less acceptable*

297–8 *(Overleaf) Theatregoing also had its attractions: the royal family enjoy themselves at the Command Performance at the Palladium in 1935 and (less obviously) at the Royal Opera House, Covent Garden, in 1946*

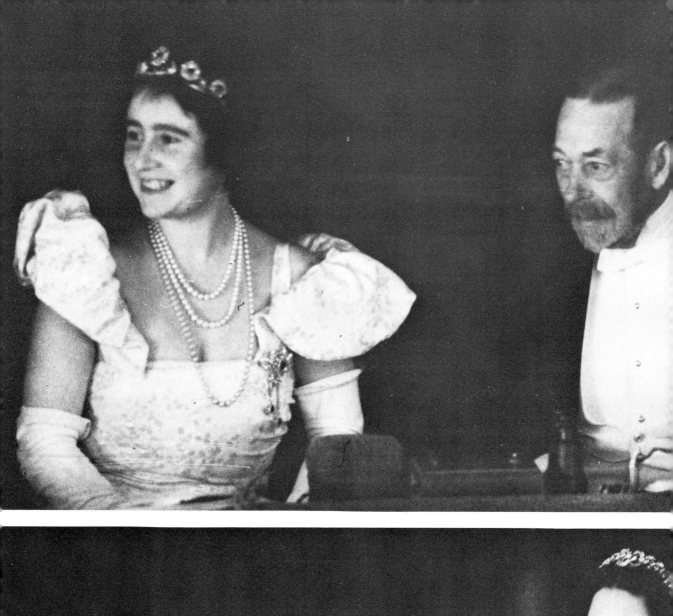

299–301 *The new generation of royals reflect modern sporting interests. Princess Anne learns to ski at Val-d'Isère; Prince Michael of Kent laps Brands Hatch at 100 mph; Prince William of Gloucester, a keen skier and flyer, was to be killed in an air race at the age of thirty*

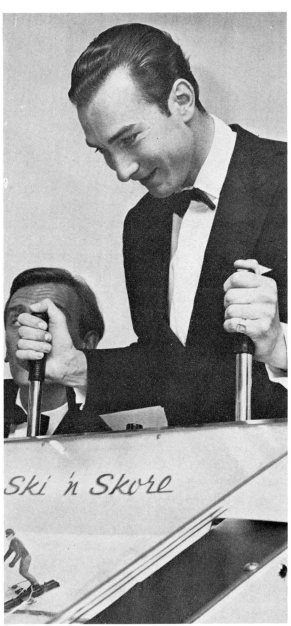

Ski 'n Skore

Chapter Seven

Splendid Isolation

Although the British monarchy has been stripped of its political power, subjected to the scrutiny of journalists, criticized in the House of Commons, mocked in cartoons and satirized on television, it is still able to provoke a certain awe. Few would nowadays claim that anything like divinity surrounds a king; nonetheless a mystique remains despite the revealed intimacies and trivialities of the BBC television film *Royal Family*, despite the monarch's voice being borne by radio waves to the farthest recesses of the globe, despite the unlidded eye of the live television camera revealing the smallest royal twitch or tremor.

The mystique rests in part upon the antiquity of the monarchical institution and the almost unbroken chain of succession stretching back to the years before the Norman Conquest; it also rests in part upon the spectacular ceremonial exaltation of the monarch and the deference habitually paid to him and to his family. Because of the nature of his position, the monarch must also endure a frequent sense of isolation, even in a crowd, for only he, upon the appointed day, can make the speech from the throne that begins the Parliamentary session, can cut the tape that opens a new bridge, can tap the foundation stone in place. If his voice falters, if his hand trembles, if his foot slips, thousands, possibly millions, of his subjects will soon know it.

Those members of the House of Windsor who have succeeded to the throne have been all too well aware of the crushing burdens of the office. George V was at least given eighteen years to adjust to his fate after the death of his elder brother Albert Victor in 1892; George VI was bustled into kingship in December 1936, and complained to his cousin Lord Louis Mountbatten: 'Dickie this is absolutely terrible. I never wanted this to happen; I'm quite unprepared for it. David [King Edward VIII] has been trained for this all his life.' Prince Charles has publicly admitted that the realization that he was heir to the throne was 'something which dawns on you with the most ghastly inexorable sense'.

There are naturally some advantages in inheriting the crown. For example even the most banal of conversational initiatives or the dullest of speeches will be listened to in a respectful, and probably attentive, silence. King George V often gave vent, in private, to the most vehement criticisms of twentieth-century degeneracy, and there were none to gainsay him – except his oldest friend, and equerry, Sir Charles Cust. There are, however, disadvantages even in respectful silences; once the young Prince Edward (the future King Edward VIII) tried in vain to interrupt Edward VII's mealtime conversation; when, at last, he was told that he could speak, he said: 'It's too late now, Grandpa. It was a caterpillar on your lettuce but you've eaten it.'

The House of Windsor has always taken its duties seriously, but the cost for the monarch and his family has often been high. This was particularly true of George V and Queen

302 George V was the epitome of the conscientious monarch, and a formidable father. Here he visits the East End of London, together with Queen Mary, in the year before his death

Mary and their children. Queen Mary once said of her children: 'I have always to remember that their father is also the King.' Since her innate respect for the head of the household was combined with an undemonstrative and reserved nature, Queen Mary's children undoubtedly suffered from some deprivation of maternal affection. King George V, though an occasionally ebullient father, was more often a terrifying patriarch, demanding an impossibly high standard in behaviour and tidiness from his royal offspring.

His children were left a good deal to their nannies in their early years. The love they received from their attendants was not always of the healthiest kind; for three years Prince Edward's nurse clung to him with a neurotic possessiveness which led her to pinch him when he was about to be presented to his parents in order that the screaming child would be handed back to her the sooner; this same nurse fed Prince Edward's brother Albert so irregularly that he developed chronic gastric trouble.

Even when infant princes and princesses are attended by emotionally stable nannies they must endure prolonged periods of separation from their parents. Foreign and Commonwealth tours, in particular, have denied royal children contact with their parents for months at a time, and when the Duchess of York (the future Queen Mary) returned in 1901 from a seven and a half month voyage in the *Ophir* with her husband she recorded that 'the younger children had grown and altered so much that when I got back, they seemed like little strangers'.

But although the junior partners in the family business have, in the past, undoubtedly suffered something for their royal birth, it is the chairman of the company who is isolated most of all. The monarch must be available and zealous and uncomplaining, whether officially welcoming the President of France or keeping abreast in private of the steady stream of state papers that require perusal and signature. The motto of the Prince of Wales is '*Ich Dein*' ('I Serve'); the motto of the monarch could well be 'I serve – alone'.

303 The eldest son and heir of George V who found the role of King too burdensome to be borne alone

304 (Left) The Head of the Commonwealth attends the opening of the New South Wales parliament in Sydney

305 For the first time, in 1958, television recorded both the opening of Parliament and the Queen's Speech from the throne in the House of Lords. Never, perhaps, can the monarch have been so isolated

306 (Overleaf) State functions such as the opening of Parliament (in this case the Parliament of New Zealand) are conducted under the full glare of modern publicity. There can be no faltering of step when the eyes of the world are upon you